No more Sugarcoats and Pick-Over Remains
I want
-The Real Meat and Potatoes of Life-

What's Tied To Your YES!!!

By
RitaShay Thomas

Published by

"Breaking Barriers Through the Word of God"
www.prophetictouch.com

Cover Design & Illustration by

"Where Brand Impacts Everything"
www.natbotheedge.com

What's Tied to Your YES!!!
By RitaShay Thomas

Manufactured in The United States of America

This book or parts thereof may not be reproduced in any form, stored in a retrieval system, or transmitted in any form by any means --- electronic, mechanical, photocopy, recording, or otherwise --- without prior written permission of the publisher, except as provided by the United States of America copyright law.

Unless otherwise noted, all scripture quotations are from
The New International Version of the Bible.

Copyright © 2004 by RitaShay Thomas
Reprint 2005 All rights reserved

Library of Congress Cataloging-in-Publication Data
Thomas, Rita S.
What's Tied to Your YES / by RitaShay Thomas
p. cm.   ISBN: 0-9770-1409-6

This book is dedicated to
all of us that have asked "Why",
wondered "How?" prayed for "When?"
and have cried out "Help!"

May you be renewed in knowing that the answers are within You.

The Word of God already has a praise of acknowledgement for you

Psalms 139: 13-16

You created my inmost being; you knit me together in my mother's womb. I praise you because I am fearfully and wonderfully made; your works are wonderful, I know that full well. My frame was not hidden from you when I was made in the secret place. When I was woven together in the depths of the earth, your eyes saw my unformed body. All the days ordained for me were written in your book before one of them came to be.

And our Lord replies

Jeremiah 29:11

I know the plans I have for you," declares the LORD, "Plans to prosper you and not to harm you, plans to give you hope and a future.

CONTENTS   Page

PREFACE
When the voice of God speaks and we respond
-I-   ---
I've gone through so much in my life
-II-   ---
So here, I begin

THE BEGINNING   ... 1
It begins with the inner me shining outward
- ❖ Take off the blinders and live life in the panoramic
    - **Reflection** - What is part of the inner you that needs to shine through?
    - **Reflection** - How do you see your life as you remove outside influences and expectations and focus on You?
- ❖ The Word of God says that even in your beginning....
- ❖ You are not on a diet. You are delivered
    - **Inspiration** - *STAY IN THE GAME*
        - **Reflection** - What experiences have you had or are still having that make you feel as though you are losing the game?
        - **Reflection** - What steps do you feel you should take to be an overcomer no matter what the circumstances?

THE ROOT   ... 25
It was when I was a child...
- **Reflection** - What seeds have been planted in your life?
- **Reflection** - How have you been dealing with after affects of things that you thought were dead and gone?
    - *-You must be able to see it (the root of it all) to overcome what you see–*
- ❖ **DIVISION**

When do the roles shift? Now, a child is playing adult games on adults' terms. Who robbed you of your childhood?
- **Reflection** - What has caused a 'riff' in your relationships or your personality? (How you deal with things)
- **Reflection** - How have 'riffs' affected your life, your outlook on life as well as your challenges in life?
- ❖ The Word of God says that every seed has purpose and that to be fruitful you must Know your roots.... (Where are you connected?)

CONTENTS (continued) Page

REALIZATION ... 45
- Who are You?
  - **Reflection** – What new things –just recently- have you realized about yourself and those around you?
  - **Reflection** - How does that make you feel?
  - **Reflection** - What aspects can you capitalize on for more happiness and contentment in your life?
- Is the non-change in You delaying the real change you desire from life?
  - **Reflection** – What things have you been trying to change about you?
  - **Reflection** – Why? Will this change help you?
  - **Reflection** - Is your drive for change dependant on the acceptance of those around you?

GRACE ... 67
- When you start to change most times others notice before you truly do.
- God Is Love and God loves You

THE PROCESS ... 83
- What is 'burning off' of you?
- What has 'marinated' with you?
  - **Reflection** – What is it that you can't believe?
  - **Reflection** – Why is it 'eating away' at you?
- Understanding the 'Potter's Touch'
  - **Reflection** – What old 'temptation' is keeping you from your 'right now' revelation?
- Are you in the midst, yet ministering?
  - **Reflection** – What processes have you gone through?
  - **Reflection** – How did you change?
  - **Reflection** – What did it bring out of you that you never knew?
  - **Reflection** – How did 'your processes' make you a better person?
- WHY?
  - **Reflection** – Where has running (away from your hurt and problems) gotten you?
  - **Reflection** – Where does your misplaced Anger… Regret lie?
- Looking Back
  Inspiration – *NOTHING, BUT JESUS*

THE REVELATION ... 114
- Realize your authority and the power within
- How do you start seeing yourself the way God sees you?
  - **Reflection** – Now, Paint Your Portrait.

CONTENTS (continued) Page

MY FINGERPRINT ... 122
- ❖ My Heart and Belief in Me now and in You
- ❖ What was tied to My YES.
  Reflection – What is tied to Your YES?
- ❖ Beloved, I leave you with this.
  Inspiration – *Lord, I come humbly …*

- ଔ**ଓ** **Author Bio** ---
- ଔ**ଓ** **Blessed to be a Blessing** – Order & Booking Information ---

God is designing my life and guiding me in living the vision in which he made provision. I am being Holy Spirit led the whole way. This part of my life feels a thousand times better than all the years past. I have truly taken a major step of faith into a new spiritual atmosphere.

But there aren't enough words to express the immeasurable amount of happiness, wholeness, and freedom that I have experienced since I said YES!!!

But what was before my 'Yes' to God?

Before the strength, joy and knowledge that I am more than what I see or what others may want for me to be…

Before I knew that I have been created unique and appointed for greatness that only my Father, The Almighty Creator of All can unleash.

How did I get from THERE to HERE?
From Before to Restored…

As you turn the pages and experience circumstances that have touched our lives at one time or another, ask yourself;

What's tied to your Yes?

What's tied to your goals?

dreams

or lack there of…

What's tied to your decision?

indecision,

your hurt,

your pain,

your tears behind the smiles,

your family secrets,

your 'white lies,'

the office you,

the church you,

the 'real' you,

Your Life….

Preface
When the voice of God speaks and we respond

-I-

Oh Lord, I have gone through so much in my life. I just want to be in right order with you. - Whatever that is – Lord, I know that I don't know all the answers. I know that I can't accomplish anything without you. Please, forgive me Father and show me the path in which you have set for me. Show me what you created me to be and for what purpose in life. Please, Lord let me not miss out on what I am suppose to do to be pleasing in your sight.

As a child, through my teenage years, when I would feel heavy, all alone and at my wits end this would be my prayer. So, I knew God or did I? I knew that since I was three I would sing and dance for the Lord. I knew that even when my mom would direct the youth choir and said I was too young to sing; I would make a point to sing louder and better so God could hear me. I knew that I needed to pray before I ate and before I went to bed. I knew that Sunday was a day of rest, family and you are not suppose to work on Sunday. I knew to make a joyful noise unto the Lord – Adam and Eve – Moses – the Red Sea – Noah - David and Goliath - Jesus on the Cross and Jesus birth – I knew… but really what did I know?

Whatever it was, it wasn't known within my being, the very fabric of my spirit. I didn't understand 'spirits.' I heard of them. I didn't know really about consecration, fasting and praying without ceasing. I just knew communion was every first Sunday and every woman wore white. However, as I grew, I tried to learn life with my patchwork of religion, good, bad, right and wrong. I was constantly searching, but for what? Love? To belong?

Why, can't I be in the clique, Lord? I get along with all of them, yet I'm tied to none. Why, can't I just go the way everyone else is going? Why, even when I try to take the back, I'm pushed to the front? Why? Why, when I try to treat others as I would want to be treated, I'm treated worse than others? Why, when I have observed others mistreat people like they could care less, they get showered with gifts and attention? Lord, what's missing? Why, when I have a question about God, I am being put down or more interrogated than understood? What is really going on?

Our Lord replies:

"Before I formed you in the womb I knew you, before you were born I set you apart; I appointed you as a prophet to the nations." "Ah, Sovereign LORD," I said, "I do not know how to speak; I am only a child." But the LORD said to me, "Do not say, 'I am only a child.' You must go to everyone I send you to and say whatever I command you. Do not be afraid of them, for I am with you and will rescue you," declares the LORD.

- Jeremiah 1:4-8

-II-

I did not ask for this. I did not ask to be minister, pastor, teacher, evangelist, prophet. I did not. When I received, 'the call,' to ministry from God, I did not want the responsibility. I knew that the Lord was moving in a great way. I was getting spiritually stronger and more aware than ever. But, me, a mouthpiece of God, one who receives a message from God and proclaims it for a specific audience -- Me!?

No, I was just fine in my box of complacency and unconfortability, pay check to pay check, overworked, underpaid, more bills than money, dysfunctional family, sit in your cubical and overeat, 4pm 'Oprah' empowerment, 5pm local news let-down, "Woman Thou Art Loosed" until the conference leaves town, "the Bishop said" prophet, email saint.

God, you can't possibly mean me "to feed your sheep?" Me?! Called from the Lord, but haven't you seen my mess, my lies, my faults, my sins, my very being? Why me? I am not worthy. But, the Lord says that your steps are ordered and it's already finished.

So, just as a builder builds a house and takes a layout of the land, there is always a picture of the finished work. God says, "I see the finished; so, I can lead you through this building process." All the time, God was saying, "Come." I was saying, "Don't you see me?" God said. "Yes, I made you." (I CHOSE the Lot) Yet, I would reply, "Don't you see my scars and residue of pain?" God says, "Yes, I placed promise inside of you." (I AM tilling the soil and planting seeds) I confess, "Lord, I look a mess." God says, "Yes, through each experience, I'm strengthening you." (I AM plotting the course) I say, "Yes, but how?" God says, "I made the blueprint." (I AM your foundation) I proclaim. "Lord, I need work; yet, I come!" God speaks and says, "With each experience your knowledge builds wisdom." (I AM setting the frame)

Before I know it, I am not who I used to be. God has built me up and made me strong. The friends I used to have I no longer have. The things I use to do, I no longer do. People, who use to have their affect on me, can't touch me. I am no longer that old person. I am a new creation in God.

A change has come and is still coming. Only God brought it about and brought me out. Easy, never will I say that the walk of sanctification is easy. Yet, it is more than anything this world can give you. Who rocked you to sleep in the midst of your tears? Who protected you from harm of sickness and your other hidden fears? No one, but God, knows your beginning and end. Yet, as I write, I ask why to my Lord. Why me? Why now?

Our Lord replies:

"Get yourself ready! Stand up and say to them whatever I command you. Do not be terrified by them. For God did not give us a spirit of timidity, but a spirit of power, of love and of self-discipline.

- Jeremiah 1:17; II Timothy 1:7

So, God in His infinite wisdom spoke and said, "Write, out of the hurt and the pain, every scar and scrape that has hindered you and yoked you up for so very long." God spoke again and said, "And do not 'sugarcoat' your experiences, because as you went through them, there wasn't an ounce of sweetness in them. Don't be like the world that wants to see, but not see. Do, but not do. Say, but not say. Be real!"

"Real!" I reply. "All out in the open...? But, this is my stuff. Why should anyone know the hell I've been through and had yet to overcome?" "Because, my child, I have heard the cries of my people and the hurt of the land. This is the heart of my children that cry out to me everyday." God replies.

So, as I submitted and committed to the task, with every experience, every unveiling of what God showed me to expose each time, I replied, "Do you know how many people feel like this?" and God said, "YES, and this is why."

So here, I begin.

[1]

-THE BEGINNING-
It begins with the inner me shining outward

Lord, I 'm not sure where I'm beginning or where I'm ending. One thing that I do know is that everything is tied to you. My accomplishments, my dreams, my fears, my testing my trials and even the tears show up as testimony of how I've made it through. Yet, still holding on to the one thing that is never changing, which is your love and belief in me.

Lord, this year has taken me from pillar to post from belief to praise from hurt and pain to perseverance; yet, I know that it is all you. I couldn't have ever imagined that I would experience what I have within these few years, but especially this year where I have been thrown out of the boat of my securities and familiarities into the water of the unfamiliar, the unknown and the uncomfortable. Lord, where are you? Lord, I see the storm. I see the boat. I even see the water. As I come, I feel like I'm sinking. This is when I have realized that I have taken my eyes off of you and focused on things that have no power over me unless I deem them to have it.

Right now, I am at enough is enough! I have pressed Lord and prayed. I have walked by faith. I know that you are not a man that you would lie. Your word does not return to you void. Tell me how to, in the midst of everything coming apart and a haze of promise before me, know which way to go? What really do I do? Is what I am doing within your divine will and not mine?

[2]

I don't want to be categorized or even thought of as a false prophet of God filled with warm fuzzes for everyone to hear and cry over, yet nothing manifests itself within their lives or even my own. – But even as the thought - the mere words appear in print – I realize that it is just distraction trying to tell me and convince me that I am not who you have called me to be.

See, idle thinking would have me to believe that I am not worthy of your time or even your consideration and that all that I went through in life has nothing to do with you. Only, the decisions that I have made make me deserve whatever I get... Well, part of that just may be true.

Yes, the things that I experience are from the decisions that I have made or not made throughout my life. However, whatever the outcome, it was for God's glory. I overcame those things. I was able to stand when others said that I would fall. I was able to bend when others knew that I would break. In all of this, I realize that with each experience, I am suppose to take from it something that I have learned and turn each and every thing that was meant to be a negative into a positive for the up building of the kingdom of God.

That means - Yes – I have gone through relationships and battles with judgment, abuse, insecurities and other things. Through it all, now, I'm able to look and say, "Here, I am. I am stronger, bolder, and more confident in who I am. In fact, I know who I am! I am living my life instead of existing. I am no longer stuck in thinking that nothing is to change -

-The Beginning-

that it's just too late for my hopes, my dreams or believing in me."

One thing I have learned, no one is going to take you to your destiny and promise, but you. No one can birth a vision that has been within your heart, but you. You have the passion! You had the experiences that took you from hurt to healing – from skeptic to believing that something must be done and that things can change. You are the one that wakes up in the middle of the night with thoughts of greatness, and you shrug it off as a good thought as you go back to sleep. You are not even realizing the inner you crying out. Who longs for peace in the midst of hell? Who longs for understanding, true change and accomplishment? Your inner power wakes you from your slumber to tell you that there is such a bigger picture here - one that is bigger than anything that you've ever known.

Has this ever happened to you? You are at work minding your own business, and someone who you barely know will come sit with you and share with you their inner-most thoughts and problems. Believe it or not, you know just where they are. You can relate to their situation and have words of encouragement for them. You find yourself empowering them with nuggets of knowledge you have gained throughout your stumbles, as well as accomplishments; and now, you can send them on their way with a better understanding that things can be better.

Think it not strange that unique instances like this happen to you. In your experiences, you were being trained for the tasks, to be equipped when ready for situations as they arise

~The Beginning~

to show growth, healing and to proclaim, "Yes, I to can overcome!"

It's funny what we accomplish when enough is enough. How many more times am I going to listen to the lies and deal with the abuse from others? How many times will I make excuses for other people and their behavior when I know better? How long is it going to take for me to know that I am more that a conqueror, the head and not the tail, above and not beneath? I was made and destined for greatness, to live with serenity, and be able to overcome any obstacle that stands in my way. I need to go through life seeing the whole picture and not being boxed in by anything or anyone. I was meant to be love exuding and to receive love back truly.

-The Beginning-

[5]

Take off the blinders and live life in the panoramic

A beautiful day, I awake and I'm already on, "Oh... I'm late," mode. I wake the children, get them ready, and check on my husband and then maybe, in the very last 5 to 3 ½ minutes, get myself together for another day of work, school, come home and work again. I soon drop the children off at school, looking like they just stepped out of a catalog. Away, I'm off in traffic rubbing my head, trying to see my way through rush hour as my husband calmly drives to work without a care in the world.

I get to work, feeling not the best, and looking not the best, yet with a little lip gloss, a brush of the hair and a smile I'll be fine. See, here is where I thrive and have just a moment of peace even while it's hectic. Here, I'm not mommy or someone's wife. I am my own person on my own terms. People see me for what I do and for who I am right now. They don't see the 'me' of yesteryear coupled with what I should have been, what I use to do and what has been said about me. I am me. I am 'the me' I strive to be, I desire to be, the no nonsense, the knowledgeable, the organized, 'problems solved' me.

Isn't it funny, that when you are at work and faced with a problem you will usually strategically find the way to fix the problem -the best line of defense- and you are able to speak with boldness and confidence; because, you know your efforts. You know your worth to the company, and you will not let anything threaten that.

~The Beginning~

[6]

Okay, let's now look at the other side of the coin. Why is it, when we are faced with the same opposition within our private lives, we allow other aspects of our personality to overtake us. Whether it is timidity, control, pride, selfishness or selflessness, we tend not to just look at the situation for what it truly is. We get caught up in feelings and how would they feel or what would they think or thoughts of you're not going to do this to me. So, there is no wavering on either part.

This reminds me of a time when we used to say we agree to disagree. Really!?! What does that mean? What you really are saying, is that, I agree that I will have my view and you will have your view. Even though, I don't agree with you and don't want to see your point. I will rather put it away and not talk about the subject since you can't see things my way. (Not good) Or better yet, let's take the more 'politically correct' approach. We don't agree on a certain subject and it's not going to make us or break us so why not drop it. But still, why don't you agree? What are your views and theirs? What is the *real* point?

Because there are various ways to get to a destination; however, if you are stuck in thinking that your path is the only way -the only solution- then you will go through life with these blinders missing the enormous panoramic view of possibilities that could help guide you and direct you throughout many aspects of life.

What should be said is, "I respect your view and I understand your point." Isn't that the real purpose of any argument or conversation, for us all to get our points across? The deliverance of the message may be different, but that doesn't mean that there is something wrong with it. If that was the case, then why use any other means of transportation than a car or any other means of sending a message than by the US postal system?

It is about a broader picture and bigger views of life and purpose that can help everyone grow. –not prove you wrong– This is to get you to the place of constantly expanding your views, strengthening your knowledge and building up the confidence so you can and will accomplish and understand anything that is thrown your way. Now, you see the panoramic view of possibilities and not the boxed in views that hinder growth.

You know, there is this channel on TV that I used to watch religiously. I mean, you better not touch my channel. I used to talk to my friends while watching the same channel, and we would put in our two cents, yet still watch, compare and be that station's 'AMEN choir' to every program.

Then, one day I just had to stop. I thought about it and started to see myself in those shows. I started to think that the life I saw in the TV shows must be the way life is or what I must expect. I thought about what it was saying to me, and it was speaking volumes. My friend would call and say, "Girl, did you just see that?" I would tell her, "I'm not watching that anymore." She would ask me, "Why?" I said, "I'm tired of seeing women being raped, beat up, mistreated, killed, molested, overlooked, abused, cheated on, disrespected and going through." All for what?! Even when it gets to the 'happy ending' is it really happy? So these episodes are showing me that in my lifetime, I'm going to either experience or know someone who has been raped, beat up, mistreated, killed, molested, overlooked, abused, cheated on, disrespected and going through…?

I started to get frustrated, thinking, well I guess this is my life. My pain, my mess. I guess you got to go through something. Life isn't perfect. You can't expect every day to be like peaches and cream. Who wrote that stuff and made sure that it is in the very fabric of relating to things as we grow? Where's the empowerment, the up building, the possibilities of promise that there is a giant in all of us. (Outside of an infomercial) Where are those everyday quotes of positivity that you can just roll off of the tongue? (Outside of a scripture) Even though those phrases are not scripture, most people know those sayings before, 'press towards the mark of a higher calling' *(Philippians 3:14)* or 'I am the righteousness of God.' *(2 Corinthians 5:21) -Scriptures paraphrased-*

Why is it, when you purchase a car, home, etc. people try to tell you what you desire or need? Or, at work there may be someone telling you what you can/cannot handle or what they think you are or are not ready for. Whose box are you putting me in?

You just have to awaken the giant inside of you. There is such a brilliant light waiting and wanting to shine from within. But first, you must acknowledge that you have a light worth shining. Every talent and gift that you have is meant to enable you to be more that a conqueror in every area in your life.

-The Beginning-

What's Tied to Your Yes

[9]

I refuse to continue to allow myself to get absorbed in things that tell me that I am suppose to be inferior to many aspects in life.

So, no! I will not accept that view of me, because it's blinded and I live my life in the panoramic.

-The Beginning-

Matthew 24:12
For whoever exalts himself will be humbled, and whoever humbles himself will be exalted.

Don't you know that every beginning is destined for a unique journey towards unforeseen experiences that lead to an unconceivable promise?

Let me tell you about David, son of Jessie of Bethlehem
(As told in I Samuel chapter 16 through II Samuel chapter 2 ending at verse 7)

He was an outcast - placed in the back with the sheep. He was not even considered by his father when Samuel came to anoint one of Jessie's sons for King. Don't you know that even in the midst of Jessie's issues and mess, God revealed to all what He called David to be – and in the midst, the least likely (David) was anointed as King.

- Further down the road – David is a child bringing his brother lunch during wartime. The least likely (David) with what you won't think could beat the opponent (a sling-shot) becomes the one that knocks down the opposition (The Giant) with a rock and kills him (The Giant) with the very thing (The Giant's sword) that he (The Giant) was going to use to kill him. (David)

- Further down the road - The Lord causes a King (Saul) to have an intolerable attitude (an evil spirit)– so much so that the people around him prayed for someone who could soothe him and comfort him –

-The Beginning-

**You must know that what you walk in (your spirit) others will see and it will precede you. **

- Before you know it, David (the forgotten one – the one no one cared to love, take under their wing, train and teach) is now in the Kings palace as his armor bearer.

- Further down the road, David was an awesome warrior with a heart for God. Even through the trials and tests, he stood his ground. He kept his focus on God; and David, became King of the very Kingdom he was serving under.

So, don't think that you have to be stuck in your beginning. Realize that it is only your beginning, training you and pulling out of you, the determination and strength you will need as you continue on to the next level into your destiny.

~The Beginning~

What hat part of the inner you needs to shine through?

-The Beginning-

[13]

How do you see your life as you remove outside influences and expectations and focus on You?

_____
_____
_____
_____
_____
_____
_____
_____
_____
_____
_____
_____
_____
_____
_____
_____
_____
_____
_____
_____
_____
_____

-The Beginning-

[14]

The Word of God says that even in your beginning....

In the beginning was the Word, and the Word was with God, and the Word was God. He was with God in the beginning. Through him all things were made; without him nothing was made that has been made. In him was life, and that life was the light of men.
- John 1:1-4

God created the heaven and the earth. A land which the Lord cares for: the eyes of God are always upon it, and, The Lord has laid the foundation of the earth; and the heavens are the works of His hands. Thy word is true and every one of thy righteous judgments endures for ever.
- Genesis 1:1; Deuteronomy 11:12; Hebrews 1:10 and Psalms 119:160

Have ye not known? Have ye not heard? Hath it not been told you? Have ye not understood from the foundations of the earth? Better is the end of a thing than the beginning thereof: and the patient in spirit is better than the proud in spirit.
- Isaiah 40:21 and Ecclesiastes 7:8

We are bound to give thanks always to God for you, brethren beloved of the Lord, because God has from the beginning chosen you to salvation through sanctification of the Spirit and belief of the truth.
- 2 Thessalonians 2:13

Though thy beginning was small, yet thy latter end should greatly increase. This month shall be unto you the beginning of months: it shall be the first month of the year to you.   - Job 8:7 and Exodus 12:2

For, I am Alpha and Omega, the beginning and the end, says the Lord, which is, and which was, and which is to come, the Almighty.
- Revelation 1:8

Just Think: Who knows you better than He who created it all?

-The Beginning-

What's Tied to Your Yes

[15]

You are not on a diet. You are delivered

There are many things going on in this world. Sometimes, I wonder am I supposed to stop and take notice, or take cover. When watching the news and all of these new reality shows, you wonder really, what is reality? I see nothing that shows what I feel or what I go through.

There was once a time in my life where I really just wanted 'right' in my life. I took the knowledge that I knew about God, mixed with all my outside influences, and became this overly worried, depressed, "I've curse my life or my life must be cursed" person.

What was strange was, while I was taking this (need more) approach, I never once thought about picking up the Bible or really trying to understand the Spirit of God or even myself. There would be times when I would try to affirm myself. I would try to explain how I felt or what I was experiencing to the fullest only for someone to take bits and pieces of what I said and change it into a totally different thought, that was not close to what I was trying to explain. I was frustrated, trying to please what I thought 'God wanted' and what would make others happy. I was constantly trying to figure everything out. I was even at my wits end.

I had this view, that in order to be one with God or to be Holy. I had to go without all the enjoyment of life. I had to become this stiff and stuffy 'Hallelujah' dress wearing all the time, look at nothing but the church channel, talk church and do church all the time person.

~The Beginning~

(This view is so far from the truth and is not scripturally based.)

God is laced throughout our everyday lives and has a wonderful sense of humor. God knows this earth and what's in it. Even though we don't have to conform to it, we also don't have to fear or run from it. God will always pull out what's inside of you in the most peculiar ways, to bless a situation right there in the midst of it all.

Have you ever tried to make changes in your life only to have others who are around you and know you tell you it won't work or that you are doing it wrong? Guess what? Forget all of that! You are at least doing something. You must realize that God is not this looming spirit looking for reasons not to bless you. On the contrary, He created you for greatness and even in your slip-ups and falls, he longs for you to realize that to truly be a conqueror in all things, is to give all of your circumstances over to Him. (Faith)

The Word of God Says:

"Do not let your hearts be troubled. Trust in God; trust also in me. (Jesus)
- John14:1

I will instruct you and teach you in the way you should go; I will counsel you and watch over you. Do not be like the horse or the mule, which have no understanding, but must be controlled by bit and bridle or they will not come to you. Many are the woes of the wicked, but the Lord's unfailing love surrounds the man who trusts in him.
- Psalms 32:8-10

Faith is the substance of things hoped for, the evidence of things not seen.
- Hebrews 11:1

-The Beginning-

What's Tied to Your Yes

[18]

-The Beginning-

INSPIRATION

STAY IN THE GAME

When you watch a game and a player has the ball,
The other team does not just let them get to the goal to score...

There is opposition and testing to get to the place where the goal can be made. The determinating factor is when the player decides how badly he wants it. This in turn, makes him plan on how he's going to play the game. Is he going to fake or stutter-step, jump-over or flip? **What will it take to make it to the goal?**

If he is the star of the team, then instead of just one opposing force there may be two or three that try to prevent him in accomplishing his task, which is to make the goal.

God is saying that as you go through, **you have said, "Yes, Lord... Use Me.... Your Will and Your Way... I just want to do what You've called me to do."**

-The Beginning-

You have just asked for the game ball and now you are on the playing field headed toward your victory. But along the way, there's going to be opposition (people saying) Did you really hear from the Lord? People telling you that you are not what you think or say that you are... In the world, we call that during a game "trash talking" and then as you make it past the half-way mark, you can already see yourself crossing over into your promise. Here come more stumbling blocks –more than one- to try and hinder you and delay your progress.

You see, they couldn't stop you when you started. So now, they had to call for backup. But the Lord said that He would take your stumbling blocks and make them your stepping stones and that He would make your enemy your footstool. So, there is no need to tarry or be weary in well doing.

Now, it is that third or forth down,
The enemy is doing the "trash talking" and has made sure that you are double-teamed.

As you line up and see the game clock
- **[The time limits that we set on ourselves]**-

Then you get weary –you just don't know how it can be done – and you see that you've lost yardage. It seems as though the enemy just might have gotten the best of you. So coach **[God Almighty]** sends in the reserves.

The players that He uses as secret weapons

-The Beginning-

- **[Holy Spirit – spiritual weapons of war]** -
They come in and they give you that peep talk
– **[You're praying now]** -
Now the play has been set
– **[You're walking in Faith now]** -
Now the whistle blows and **the Lord is saying, "Come"**

Even though it doesn't look good and you don't know how you'll be able to accomplish this –

You start the play
– **[You're activating Your Faith]** -

And the Lord comes in and switches the play
- **[His thoughts are not our thoughts and His ways are not our ways]** -

Before you know it, no matter what the enemy tries to do to stop you
The game (Your Situation) just seems to take on a life of its own
– **[The favor of God is upon you]** -

You look around and your team has scored
– **[You've been blessed and your prayer has been answered]** –

Not the way in which you thought that it was going to be answered, yet God showed up and showed out. Everything that the enemy meant for bad, God had it to boomerang and work for your good.

-The Beginning-

[22]

You are walking in the 'promise' in victory because of what God has already predestined in your life

When opposition, tests and trials are going on in your life
– **Rejoice, and again rejoice!!!!**

For God has handed you the ball **(of your promise and destiny).**
It doesn't matter what the circumstances look like.

-Be like Peter and "COME" -
And know that with each step of faith,
God will solidify your foundation and direct your path.

-The Beginning-

[23]

What experiences have you had or are still having that make you feel as though you are losing the game?

-The Beginning-

[24]

What steps do you feel you should take to be an over-comer no matter what the circumstances?

_____
_____
_____
_____
_____
_____
_____
_____
_____
_____
_____
_____
_____
_____
_____
_____
_____
_____
_____
_____
_____
_____

-The Beginning-

Pet Peeves?   Chaos & Confusion?

Old Grievances?   Infidelity?

Misunderstanding?

Misplacement?   Abuse?

What was said?   What wasn't said?

Lies & Judgment?

What is rooted so deeply within you that it is hindering your momentum to breakthrough and rise above what was once beneath you?

-THE ROOT-
It was when I was a child...

Late night, sitting here at my desk and my children are finally asleep; the house is now quiet, or is it? I can still feel the lurking eyes of my mother, wanting desperately for us to be in our own space and my grandmother praying for us to be alright. I don't know about you, but I know my family is not perfect. But really, whose family is?

I was the only child and felt alone for 9 ½ years and then my brother came. Great! I have someone to love and talk too. (The thoughts of a young child) My mom worked a lot and was still trying to get her life back on track. (After my father's infidelities and fathering another child outside of their marriage) My grandmother worked, but it was inside of the house. So usually, it was just me, my thoughts and imagination as entertainment throughout each day. My grandfather was this big loveable no nonsense kind of fellow, that everyone loved, senior deacon at one of the biggest mega churches in Memphis, TN and their chief cook. So, he was always busy doing something for the church. To me, I was in a typical household where on Sunday we go to church, we eat, we sleep, not too much outward affection and go through our Monday through Saturday and start it all again.

I grew up thinking that I could never do enough to please my family. You understand, as they say –back in the day– children need to be seen and not heard. I also grew up trying to get my family reality to fit into what I would see on

TV - all smiles, lots of outwardly shown love, and every problem would have a loving 30 minute fix of understanding. (Not true -not real- and not good that I would even expect that).

I have experienced situations where I knew that I wasn't being treated right, yet I came to 'grin and bear it', expect it, okay it and settle for it. (Where's the root of it all?)

At school, I was never part of a group of people that just hung out. I always had maybe one or two close friends and that would change almost as the school years would. It was weird; because, I was friends with many people. It didn't matter where you were in life, I would always have a smile for you.

But lonely, I was sitting at home wondering, where's my dad and why doesn't the other side of my family ever call me? We all are in the same city and nothing. Sometimes, I would get so lonely, that I would go through the phone book and call every person with my last name until I found someone related to my dad and then I would ask if he was there and what was his number.

BREAK Look at the seed being sown. Already at an early age, I was teaching myself how to chase after something/someone that doesn't have that same desire towards me. I am already devaluing myself. This starts the mentality of the encouraging cheerleader of everyone or the extreme skeptic. Everyone is worthy, but you. Help them to reach their goals and procrastinate or downplay your own. Or, the extremist who says, "What makes them so special?" Or, the over compensator/challenger/super-

competitor, who wants to prove you wrong or show you up. Either way the inner-hurt says, "I don't belong and I am on the backburner." These feelings will continue to be a tumor in and around things in your life until you deal with them, remove the residue of pain, and see it for what it is.
Old hurt trying to poison the present you.***

Even when the years would pass and it began to seem obvious that on both sides I came at the wrong time, I know my mom's side of the family loved me; but, what about dad's?

Funny how life is from relationship-to-relationship and from experience-to-experience, there are things that I will touch on that I have experienced and it is to hurt no one, but to get to the root of things and to say enough is enough of sugarcoats, and saying, well it really didn't go that way. I'm sick and tired of people in bondage of yesteryear, living life with blinders and not the panoramic, walking through life on auto-pilot and not really guiding yourself and your thoughts towards the destiny that you were meant to have.

Aren't you tired of the same-stuff, different-day routine? The girlfriend conversation ('If it were me, girl'...) must stop. Well, guess what? It's not just you, but we all need something to bring us out and through. We must not continue in this every day excuse of day – month – year - weekend party – club – beer – repent - back to work and the cycle continues again type of thinking.

How many times do we have to be hurt and deceived by the same people, but in different bodies over and over and over again? I hope this pattern, today, is broken as you heal through this journey of revelation and self preservation to get to higher-heights knowing that greatness is within your reach.

It's one thing to read something or to even hear something...

But to **apply it** to your life is something totally different.

Always Remember

When YOU change your **Thinking**,

YOU change your **Beliefs**.

When YOU change your **Beliefs**,

YOU change your **Expectations**.

When YOU change your **Expectations**,

YOU change your **Attitude**.

When YOU change your **Attitude**,

YOU change your **Behavior**.

When YOU change your **Behavior**,

YOU change your **Performance**.

When YOU change your **Performance**,

YOU change your **LIFE!**

-The ROOT-

What's Tied to Your Yes

[30]

What seeds have been planted in your life?

How have you been dealing with the after affects of things that you thought were dead and gone?

– You must be able to see the root of it all to be able overcome what you see –

_____
_____
_____
_____
_____
_____
_____
_____
_____
_____
_____
_____
_____
_____

Just Think: If you hide from your hurt or tuck it away, it can always one day return, reveal itself and hurt you just like the first time   –Because you never dealt with it –

-The ROOT-

-DIVISION-

When do the roles shift? Now, a child is playing adult games on adults' terms.
Who robbed you of your childhood?

Hot summer day and all seems well. I'm wearing denim shorts and a navy blue shirt with some type of logo that I thought was cuter than I cared about what it meant. There I am on the porch with my grandfather cutting the hedges and the other neighborhood kids going to and fro from each others houses and the candy lady, etc. I already knew that it wasn't for me, because I wasn't allowed. Never the less, I sat and observed people, their outfits, cars, birds and how the sun danced upon one roof top and cascaded to the trees and faded on the lawn. I just sat and watched and relaxed and like a gust of wind they came....

This white "family vacation" overly packed station wagon. I didn't know who they were. Low and behold, in and up our driveway, they came. My grandfather waited and then they greeted each other. I didn't know if they were family or friend. The wife and kids came pilling out to the car like a monsoon, they overtook me and the peace that I was in and our home. Then, the grown-ups were all inside talking about the good old days, the other son was engulfed in food and television, and the oldest brother was outside on the porch with me. Odd, I thought, since the youngest brother was closest to my age of ten.

[34]

This guy was tall, well groomed, slim, well spoken, and 15. He complimented me constantly. I wasn't used to that. He talked about my voice, my eyes, my lips, and even my shape. I felt flushed, but I didn't know what I felt – funny – flattered or just flustered – No one had ever talked to me like that or ever looked at me the way he looked at me. I didn't know whether to go inside with the adults or stay outside. I mean, he was talking nice and to hear those things about ME was unusual, but very nice.

Then we went inside and the adults were still talking, cooking, laughing and joking etc. His brother was doing his thing and just did not want to be bothered. It was like -you know- we were set apart from everything and everyone.

Then, he touched me and a heat went through my body. I felt embarrassed. As I tried to discretely walk away, he pulled me close and his body touched mine and he kissed me! Me!

I pulled away. – Flushed with fear and confusion - What is happening? What are we doing? This is so much so fast, I couldn't find my grounding. He complemented me again and even asked if anyone had ever made me feel this way. "No." I faintly replied. I felt like I was in an old musical. Is this love? Am I crazy? Is he family? I could hardly remember anything except that I felt weak, confused, afraid and naïve all in one. Then, he led me to the restroom.

There, I thought okay. He'll wait for me outside while I can figure out what's going on, wash my face and calm down. My whole body was flushed, but he didn't wait outside. He came inside and locked the door.... Then he.... OHH OUCH!!! I almost screamed. He pulled his fingers back, held his head and said, "You have never done anything like this?" Like a child feeling like I had been caught with something, I said, "No." He looked disappointed. After all that was going on and my body trying to calm down, he shook his head. I didn't understand what was wrong or what just happened, but to see him not as excited or happy about me, I felt like I had disappointed him. So, I started to tear up and say I'm sorry.

BREAK Another seed is being planted. This seed has you conform to events even when uncomfortable. This seed has you to submit fully to the opposite sex and apologize even though you know that you've done nothing wrong. This usually transforms one to becoming a 'yes person' or over compensator. If I don't do it no one will. One feels guilty to deny anyone even if it puts you at a disposition. ***

He immediately said, "Sorry, for what, don't be sorry. You just aren't ready and I can wait..." (Even though his body language was saying something totally different) He kissed my forehead and looked at me. I thought in my mind, he meant wait for me or that this wasn't the last time I would see him. I thought the thoughts of a child. After all of this, after all he's shown me and "how he cares" he won't abandon me.

I walked out of the bathroom and he tried to pull me back saying, "Let's do this"... Not even a minute from when he spoke again, our names were being called. I went one way through the house and he went another. By it being such a big house, no one ever thought anything more about it.

The rest of the day, we made eyes at each other from across the room, but that was that. Then, it was time for his family to leave. I felt sad, but then again I was still trying to keep myself in line. I gave everyone a hug as they were leaving out. When I gave him his hug he said, "Remember me." "I will." I said faintly and they left. To this day I have never seen him again.

After they left, I went to my room and closed the door. I keep playing the days events over and over in my mind. Every now and then, my body would warm up just by thinking about it. I took some paper and stared to write his name and that I loved him over and over and then I took the paper and slept with it.

The next morning was very different, I felt strange, my body felt strange. When I would think about what had happened the day before, I would feel dirty and lost. I felt stupid and when I tried to think of his last name, I didn't know it. I calmly asked my grandmother what was their address. She said that she didn't know and there was no need for me to be writing no boys anyway at my age.

I felt like I was in this box of misunderstanding and confusion. And from what I knew about GOD and what I didn't understand about myself, I thought that I had cursed myself or sinned. So, I felt horrible. I had no one to speak to; because, I was too embarrassed. I didn't know what to say or how to say it. Because, willing I went and willing I waited, but for what?

> **NOTE:** I'VE LEARNED THAT EVERY ABUSER ISN'T ALWAYS VIOLENT. THEY AREN'T ALWAYS POSSIBLE STRANGERS OR EVEN ADULTS. THEY COME IN ALL SHAPES AND SIZES. THEY TRY TO GAIN CONFIDENCE IN WHO THEY DESIRE TO ABUSE AND/OR MANIPULATE. IN THAT, THEY CAN HAVE AMPLE OPPORTUNITIES TO ABUSE AGAIN AND AGAIN, WITH A FALSE SENSE OF CONFIDENCE THAT THEY WON'T BE FOUND OUT.

So this chapter of my life, I vowed to close and forget, to try and forgive myself and let it go, but the residue of the experience tracked me, haunted me, and wrestled with me, year after year until God had me to pull it back up in remembrance and truly cleanse myself with the Word of God in discerning and purging things that were not of HIM from my past so that I could move on from it.

You know I wondered after remembering this:

#1 – Why did I need to share this experience?
#2 – Why did it go the way that it did?
#3 – Why didn't I put up a fight?
#4 – Why was I so receptive?

Where is <u>the root</u> of this?

Then one night, I was awakened by a vision from my past. I was 2 not even three years old. I was with -I guess- my babysitter. I remember the park and the swings and that we were walking from there to the inside of the apartments. (the kind were you walk in a door that closes then you can either go into the downstairs or upstairs apartments from there) There in the hallway, were other teens her age. I couldn't

~The ROOT~

understand what they were saying, but there was this boy who couldn't have been older than me and the teens gathered around us and pulled our pants down and laid me down and pushed him on top of me. I didn't like it. So, I screamed, "No!" and pushed him off. He hit me in the face. I cried. Some of the teens laughed and then the babysitter hurried me home. She told me never to say anything about it or my mom will spank me for being bad. When we arrived home and my mom asked what's wrong, the babysitter said that I had fallen. All I could do was cry. As my mom went through thanking her, she asked me, "Where did it hurt and didn't she tell me to watch were I'm going?"

That was the seed. This is what I received from it, if approached in uncomfortable situations with the opposite sex, don't react just accept it. By doing that, you'll be liked not made fun of and not hurt. I also thought that I should be ashamed of things that happen to me even if I didn't bring them on. So, I learned to bottle my feelings up as to protect others, because I won't be protected or believed. This is dangerous, because this is what starts the calm to explosive process. People who seem to take everything in -the ones that are a little too patient -that seem to be too understanding -too compromising and one day something breaks the silence, the patience and everything uncontrollably explodes.

I wrestled with that all the way through my childhood/teens and into my thirties until God cleansed me of the residue of that experience.

Now, I can tell you about my hurt and not be tainted by it.

-The ROOT-

What's Tied to Your Yes

What has caused a 'riff' in your relationships or your personality (How you deal with things)?

~The ROOT~

[40]

How have 'riffs' affected your life, your outlook on life as well as your challenges in life?

Life's Challenges…and What now?

Isn't it strange how, you never really sit back and think about your life; mainly because, we really don't want to confront the many things that have hurt us and that we allowed. The very thought that we may be carrying around some of that very same hurt now, may make us feel more defeated and ashamed than feeling as someone who has overcome the circumstance.

When I was 12, doctors told my mother and I after my check up and some tests that I would never have children. Well, even at 12 it came as quite a blow. Yet, I still didn't get the full understanding of it. A few years passed and then like a wave rushing towards the tide at 16, I hungered to be a mother. Not understanding what I was thinking of or saying. I was very serious about it. Why? I was hurting. I felt misunderstood and unwanted. I felt like a hindrance and a burden to my family and even to my friends. I wanted to fill that void. No matter what the intentions were from whom I was seeking attention from, it didn't matter. I could 'love' enough for the both of us. I started skipping school (something I never did before). I thought that I had a boyfriend who loved me -but no- he (like so many other young boys) just wanted to have sex. (By any means necessary)

My first time was unexpected and afterward I didn't feel 'womanly'. I felt dirty and confused with my mind filled with a tinted image of love and lovemaking and how it could be. I then started to put him on a pedestal that he didn't deserve. No matter how he treated me, talked to me, or how uncomfortable he made me feel, I took it and figured if I just loved him more it would be different. No! No!! No!!! Through the lies, the cheating and deceit, I hung on like an unhappy addict not understanding that this misery could end and the illusion of love that I thought I had was not love at all.

Relationship after relationship, I swore I would never go through that again. Yet, with each new relationship, I did more, I gave more and I hurt more until I decided I'm just not going to care. So, I just dealt with it. I made excuses on their behalf. I would say things like, "He's misunderstood... He's going through... You just don't know him like I do." All of those excuses were just a smoke screen, and for what? I was hiding from others what I already knew. I really didn't want to admit to myself that I had settled and lowered my standards until there were no standard at all. Before I knew it, I was a puppet listening to who I allowed to pull the strings feeling that there was no way out. I did not give myself credit that I had my own mind, my own dreams, my own aspirations and my own goals. All of that was just a distant memory. All I could see were the pictures that they painted of me that seem to dim the light shinning on better realities for me. I started using vises to dull the pain. I started to wonder, 'how did I get here,' and believe that I couldn't see my way out.

You see, I started to hate intimacy. It seemed as, the satisfaction was always theirs and I'm left feeling obligated longing to hold on to any hint of acceptance and love they could give me. I did not understand that I connected to someone that spiritually I never was meant to be joined too.

After high school then college, my thinking had changed on a lot of things. I dated this guy who was an achiever. He accomplished things. "If I only could have taken more of an interest in me, who knows," I use to say. He was what I used to call 'too nice.' The problem is that there is no such thing.

You know, the very people that God blesses us with throughout our lives to help us grow and move into 'the real you' are usually the ones we condemn in some way. Usually, they are not who we expected them to be or the opportunity didn't come in the timing we thought it should come.

As this person gave me all that I had prayed for and more, I let others influence me and pull me away. I allowed the influence of others and what was said and thought dictate my choices, MY DECISIONS. I ended up down many dead ends, many tearful nights and many questions why. I *allowed* others to dictate *my walk*, never realizing that they would never have to deal with the outcome of MY decision. I put my faith in, what they said, more than who I am.

The Word of God says that every seed has purpose and that to be fruitful you must KNOW your roots....
Where are you connected?

John 15:1-4

"I am the true vine, and my Father is the gardener. He cuts off every branch in me that bears no fruit, while every branch that does bear fruit he prunes so that it will be even more fruitful. You are already clean because of the word I have spoken to you. Remain in me, and I will remain in you. No branch can bear fruit by itself; it must remain in the vine. Neither can you bear fruit unless you remain in me.

Ephesians 3:17-18

May your roots go down deep into the soil of God's marvelous love. And may you have the power to understand, as all God's people should, how wide, how long, how high, and how deep his love really is. (NLT)

GOD is LOVE

Take flight in your life with options and opportunities that are
Endless

-REALIZATION-
Who are you?

Lord, you said it and it shall be. I feel such a peace and then again a reawakening of spirit. You are right. If I stand for nothing then really what do I stand for and for what purpose? What do I believe in and for what cause? I know Lord that you deal with me in a very unique and beautiful way. You have awakened senses in me that I never knew as well as principles in me that I have always known, but never executed.

It amazes me when I think about the many times that I would actually visualize myself singing before crowds, talking a long walk, sticking to an eating plan, saying no to someone and really showing my strength by sticking to it.

As I ponder, a thought comes to mind of how my life has taken a total turn since I laid down my life and chosen God's plan, His will and His way. It hasn't been easy. In fact, as I journey, I have realized that the more of my purpose God would reveal to me the more of my past I would consider and even compare which would hinder me. With each unveiling like a flower blooming, God would pull back each layer of beauty and each speck of mess and show me the pureness of His love, the peace in His power and the life within His grace. So, I come in faith knowing that God won't lead me astray.

-REALIZATION-

[46]

Consistency. Discipline. Dedication to myself is the revelation that my Father and Lord has revealed to me. I can not continue to bear the burdens of the world, try to solve all problems, fix all hurt and cheer and empower everyone but me. I must have faith, belief, truth and diligence in all God has shown me and is continuing to show me about me. I must stick to the task which is to get in the game, believe in my abilities, run the play, visualize the victory, activate my faith and cheer (the creation) myself in knowing that God has anointed and called these actions for such a time as this.

Revelation is so evident when things we once hid and once had been hidden come to light. You can look past what's seen and what's happened and pull out the lessons God gave and still gives you to surpass it. From glory to glory, God reveals and heals so as you give testimony you carry the spirit of the one who delivered, healed, redeemed, set-free, saved, called and chosen to impart and have joy in you.

In love, we must understand that even within God's principles we were meant to love God above all things, but next and also just as important to love ourselves. If we become focused only when being pushed by others then where's the standard, the drive, the boundaries that are yours and yours alone? You must take a stand and not settle or downplay your beauty, talent, wisdom or importance.

Every time you allow for your thoughts and actions to place you beneath others 'O yea of little faith.' God created you and no other like you. -For great and wondrous things- When

-REALIZATION-

you doubt yourself, you doubt God. Look up and Live life. Blessed!

How long do we plan to be a devoted fan to a game that we were meant to not only play, but win! It's time to enjoy 'the peace', enjoy 'the joy' and enjoy 'the love' of the Lord. Understand that his words are forever valid. The Lord, the creator of all things chose you. He chose the laugh, the smile, the voice, the passion, even how you relate to things, how you praise and worship. Let not one rock cry out for you when you have a voice - Use it!

Allow God to take you to that secret place, that holy place where God shines his glory and you lay down every weight. You must everyday make time for silence and meditation. Know that as each day passes, it's a day of assignment and expectation. God is in constant motion and you should be also. *IN MOTION*: in faith, in perseverance, in stretching your abilities as well as your thinking. He sees your heart.

Blessed be the name of the Lord! Every word cursed assignment, which has been spoken over your life, is now cancelled in the name of Jesus. Praise His holy name!

You should no longer allow yourself to be worn down by people trying to explain their problems and situations that have nothing to do with you, to you. They try to obligate you into becoming a crutch and an enabler, pulling you from where your focus must lie. Realize that their cross isn't for you to bear.

-REALIZATION-

Lord, I thank you for revelation knowledge. Yet, even when it is there; we have free-will. However, at times, we allow that free-will to override what really should be happening within our lives.

I know that the Lord directs, guides, shelters and covers not just me but everyone and their whole household. I use to wonder why it never seemed like I had enough time in the day. I would see other people who had much more than me on their plate, yet they seemed unfazed and more organized. How? It's called FOCUS.

Don't you hate it when people try to sum your problem up in this general fix? Let's say you're overweight and someone says, "Well, just stop eating." You want to say to them that – that is not the full sum of the issue. It may very well have nothing to do with it. They don't know your history, your feelings, and your ins and outs. If you don't know them all, then how could they possibly know? Yet, they sum you up as this out of control person that saw the problem and did nothing.

Let me share something with you. All of my life, I have dealt with people who said that I was fat and overweight. As I look back at my pictures and my lifestyle, I was healthy and perfectly fine. I was curvy and not like your teen dream pictures, but how much of a percentage of people are? So, I tried to alter myself, starve and workout more. All it did was make me insecure about myself. I started comparing myself to other people and wanting my legs to look like hers and my chest to be smaller and my butt to be tighter instead of enjoying being a healthy, beautiful, smart, intelligent, talented child. *(WHAT A SEED)* Then as I grew into adulthood, the comparisons never stopped, instead they escalated. I would find myself saying, "Well, I may not have this, but I have this. I may not be able to do that, but I am better at this."

It's sad when you enter a room and glance to see who really can compare to you before you walk in... (Not good) Then the other nuggets of life start to evolve and before you know it, other things are more important and the vanity of it all is not. However, that's how you affirmed yourself. Now, you are no longer doing what it took to maintain your vanity. Then, before you know it, stress, other things, pound, pound, hormones and more stress and then here we are – what everyone had said we would be.

What have people spoken about you that you knew was not true, and as life continued -you woke up one day and the picture they continued to paint and show you, about you– YOU were?...

Take this on for size, people who are close to you start to make jokes and put you down thinking that it will jump start you into becoming (basically not who you want to be) who they can tolerate you to be. They feel very validated in doing that.

What if you turned the tables and did the same to them? Just casually say to your mate, "Nice going there 'knobby." (Because of a portion of their body that is smaller than

-REALIZATION-

normal) Why not say to a family member that isn't that clean, –neat – "When we have the next cook-out this year just come. Because, no telling what has crawled into your food."

Do these instances sound cruel? Good! That's what has become of our society telling you that you must fit in a box that the majority of us don't fit in, and that you must be like what most of us were never meant to be.

I Samuel 16:7
The LORD does not look at the things man looks at. Man looks at the outward appearance, but the LORD looks at the heart."

Did you ever wonder why God gave everyone (including twins) different fingerprints? It has nothing to do with judge, jury, or prosecution, but just like the fingerprints where no two in the whole earth are the same, that is the same analogy for your purpose. No two are the same; there may be similarities, but not the exact same.

You have promise and greatness in you that was destined before the heavens, –before the 2nd grade spelling bee - before 'Harry met Sally' – before 'You've got mail', before silent night and the manger, before it all there you were before the Father being taught, loved and exalted.

So, why is it that we now can sit, believe and conceive a non-reality to our reality as law and condemn ourselves in the everyday mundane 'this is just the way it is' blues. No way!!!

-REALIZATION-

1 John 5:3-4; Romans 12:10

For this is the love of God, that we keep his commandments: and his commandments are not grievous. For whatsoever is born of God over comes the world: and this is the victory that overcomes the world, even our faith. Be kindly affectionate one to another with brotherly love; in honor preferring one another. (NKJV)

SEE IT!
YOUR VISION

SAY IT!
YOUR PASSION
&
MAKE IT HAPPEN!!!
YOUR PURPOSE

In everything you do, do it in excellence - without fear or fault, because it is in the spirit of God. You don't need anyone to tell you to work, to save, to be polite, to forgive, or even to excel in what you do. Your focus should not just be in the benefits, but the benefactor. God knows your heart. God knows what he placed deep down inside that is longing to come out and execute all that you were created to do. The worker never lacks. One who is busy in Kingdom works will not get caught in idol traps, because of focus.

Stay Focused and Be Free!!!

~REALIZATION~

[52]

What new things -just recently- have you realized about yourself and those around you?

___

-REALIZATION-

What's Tied to Your Yes

[53]

How does that make you feel?

-REALIZATION-

[54]

What aspects can you capitalize on for more happiness and contentment in your life?

-REALIZATION-

Is the non-change in You delaying the real change you desire from life?

I never knew what true friendships could lead to until lately. I know that through life we try to do a comparison of you scratch my back and I'll scratch yours filled with optimism and our expectations of what a friend should be. At times, our expectations may outweigh the type of friend that we really are to others.

Lord, amazing it is that even as I teach my children things each day, I see them grow and excel in things that I hadn't even touched on as well as thought of. What is so great, is that my children know that you exist and not only that you exist, but how to be grateful, thankful and how to acknowledge when they are not doing the right things and correct themselves. Why, we as adults and younger adults don't get that? We don't grasp the fact that the more you are kind – kindness comes back – the more you love – love comes back. The old saying, "If you have nothing good to say then don't say anything at all." This could alleviate so much drama in life.

Why do we criticize and talk about others when we haven't gotten ourselves together fully? If someone is having a bad day or just have a bad attitude, kindness can correct it every time. You don't have to receive into your spirit any outer mess.
    -Unless you feel like taking out the garbage today-

-REALIZATION-

I remember that there was this woman that was a cashier and she was very rude and very nasty to the customers and co-workers. I decided that I was not going to let her ruin my day. As I went up to get checked out, she had a nasty look on her face and smart remarks ready. I smiled at her. She looked at me like I was crazy. As she finished up, bagged my things and rolled her eyes, I turned back and said, "You may not know it, but you are appreciated. Goodbye."

I don't know what happened with that young lady after that, but I could feel the anger and the hurtfulness on her breaking away as I said that and walked away. I was not looking for accolades or a phone number so that I can 'lead her to the water'. Sometimes the best testimony is within your attitude. Your walk, your talk, a simple touch or hug can set someone's day better. When you let someone know that they are loved when they look down and pressured, the expression of selflessness is worth more than millions to ones spirit. God leads you to know what to say and what not to say.

One thing I have learned in ministry, everyone that God allows you to touch and minister too are not necessarily suppose to be tied to you. Understanding this helps a lot of ministers starting out. However, this overall principle is key for everyone. People that you care for, related to or work with are not necessarily tied to you. We must know when to say no. Just because I know you and have been there for you from time to time does not mean that each time you need, I am obligated to play search, retrieve and rescue for you or with you. We must understand that if we keep putting our two cents in every time we see that there is an issue then how will that person know how to stand on their on? How will they learn from their adversities? How will they develop their own stronger spirituality and maturity? How will they see how **GOD** brought them through?

I have wondered to myself what exactly is going on with us (your people). Do we really have faith? We say that we are conquerors, but why don't we learn from past lessons?

The unique thing about the thinking that goes behind these -helping out- actions is that I always said, "I just want the best for people. I don't want to see them in a jam." Yet, is it meant for me to be a part of the process that they are going through? Where does helping and enabling differ? I can tell you.

I was helping someone on the other side of town with a project. My job coming into the project was to only type up and printout the documents after final draft. Before I knew it, I was expected to do research *(because this project was really important and they didn't have all the materials and this could affect their job)* and then instead of just typing and printing, they wanted adjustments and delivery. I started to feel frustrated, but guess what? No one brought it on, but me. I could have said no. I could have just pulled out, but because I still had that –[must see you succeed no matter what the cost is to me **seed**] –in my system- I just dealt with it.

You must understand what crosses are for you to bear. Why do some people put what can or cannot happen to them on other people's shoulders? Why don't they want to take responsibility for their own processes, experiences and actions? Just because someone cares for you and is willing to help you, doesn't mean that you take the back and lay the whole idea on their shoulders waiting for it to succeed so that you can take credit or point the finger if something goes wrong. Understand that no matter what the circumstance, if it was brought to you, then you have what it takes to make it through. Even when you know that you may have someone who is willing to help, our friends and family were not put here to be crutches or enablers. We are here to encourage and grow together as we all journey through this thing called life.

I wish I knew that back when I was just starting to walk in what God had spoken over me. I would pray, counsel and minister to people. Like a tidal wave, my life was no longer my own. I didn't mind it to an extent; however, my phone was nonstop. I started to be on 24hr call and my family started to feel the tug. I didn't want someone hungry for God to feel lost or alone or misunderstood. I wanted them to see that even in the midst of pain there's a miracle waiting to happen. They just need to stop trying to figure it out and let God and their faith in God lead them in the way in which they should go.

Soon, I started to feel weary in well doing. I started to get on myself for letting myself get down. I felt drained and I was. Still as others would call for help, others would criticize saying things like, "You are not suppose to go through. You are anointed. You are called from God or are you?" I would cry out Lord, why this? I have a full plate already. I'm going through a divorce, living with my parents, no money, two children, bills, failing health, serving in ministry, striving for better, praying, fasting and helping others, sacrificing and still getting torn down by some of the very same people who in less than a week needed prayer and a prophesy. These same people would get mad at me if I told them, "I don't have a word for you. You need to press in and pray. This is the time for you to study the Word of God and He would reveal to you what to do."

I didn't understand the manipulation that was involved. I submitted and committed to the task of being a servant of God and heeding to His call until –one night – God woke me and said – NO MORE!!!

He showed me everything that was surrounding me and the old habits and traits that they were trying to reactivate in me to hinder me from doing really what I was placed here to do. As God would show me my distractions and where I was falling short, he would also show me how I pleased him and would show me my own growth. He would refresh me and fill me with his love that would be so beautiful that a weep turns to joy that rocks you to a peaceful sleep to awaken anew. That's the kind of God I serve!

Know this, even in correction God will not confuse, condemn, or discourage you from doing what is within His will. So if you have been in situations where you where trying your best for good and was condemned, confused and being told that God was unhappy with you... Always look into the scriptures and know your worth:

¹ John 4:1
Dear friends, do not believe every spirit (attitudes, thoughts, actions) but test (observe, check, examine, analyze) the spirits (attitudes, thoughts, actions) to see whether they are from God
-Scripture paraphrased-

Psalms 118:8
It is better to take refuge in the Lord than to trust in man.

God is all knowing. I have a divine call on my life and guess what so do you; but, if each time there is danger, you cry wolf and never stand and pull from within yourself to see what you can do to slay the wolf then how have you grown? How have you overcome? How have you excelled in that which you never thought you'd be able to do?

My Bishop says constantly, "Enough is enough of church, old time religion, past the plate, go home, eat, sleep and raise hell all week." It's time for you to active the gift in you and know that destiny isn't just part of an R&B group, but it's within you. It's longing to come out. It's lined up with your gifts and talents coupled with your skills and aspirations and cultivated by your pain and fears to mix and become that

-REALIZATION-

unbelievable breakthrough that you've been feeling is for you, but could never see – Until now!

One great actor once said that all of his accomplishments happened because he faced them all scared to death, but willing to see it to the end. What does that mean? That means, he is scared to fail, yet scared to achieve because of the responsibility that will be involved once the goal is achieved. Sometimes, you may just be plain scared of venturing into something that leaves you clueless of what may or may not be in the end, yet you press on.

See, that's part of the press when the unknown is so thick, but because you have faith that there is a God that sits up high and looks down low and wants the best and this is only a test, then you can reach down deep within yourself and say I can, I will and I must do this.

Every great success took risks. Every great idea took lots of criticism. Someone had to believe. Have you every known someone who has great passion, great talent and they are always talking about the shoulda, woulda, couldas of life? Yet when opportunity arises for them to possibly accomplish what they have been talking about doing all this time, there is always some kind of glitch, some kind of problem, and now the timing isn't quite right. Before, they were always saying, "If I only had this, if I only had that, then I would be happy." However, when it manifests, there is always some reason of delay. (some excuse)

-REALIZATION-

You see words have power and God hears you. A lot of times, what you say is right before your face. God has placed it at your feet. You waste time and opportunity, because it didn't come in your pre-imagined package.

***Make the Decision

<u>Not</u> an Excuse***

-REALIZATION-

What's Tied to Your Yes

What things have you been trying to change about You?

-REALIZATION-

[64]

Why?

Will this change help you?

~REALIZATION~

Is your drive for change dependant on the acceptance of those around you?

-REALIZATION-

UNDERSTAND THIS:

I AM BUT A RIPPLE WITHIN THE WAVES OF IMPARTATION THAT JESUS 'OUR ROCK' HAS TROWN INTO THE LIVING WATERS FOR US ALL TO BE REFRESHED, RENEWED AND RESTORED. MAY YOUR RIPPLE GO OUT AND BECOME BIGGER THAN MINE AND YOUR INFLENCES THROUGHOUT YOUR LIFETIME BE BIGGER THAN YOU.

John 14:12

Verily, verily, I say unto you, He that believeth on me, the works that I do shall he do also; and greater works than these shall he do; because I go unto my Father. (KJV)

-REALIZATION-

-GRACE-
When you start to change most times others notice before you truly do

He saw me!!! I was going through a terrible relationship. I had a false sense of self worth; yet, he saw me. After many days of making excuses for my mate's behavior, trying to answer - why he is not working - why he is not loving - why he won't participate in family functions – why he just won't do anything, unless it is something in which he came up with to do himself for himself. After overworking – over understanding – over loving – believing if I just get this right then he would understand; he would come to his senses about how we should be. But that was not the case, the more that I tried, the more things grew worse and the unhappy he supposedly was which gave him leeway to do things that would totally disrespect me and our union. (In review: Can you see this seed?)

I started this new job. As I was going through training, there he was... He was gorgeous with deep brown skin, wavy hair and hazel brown eyes set deep under perfectly shaped thick brows. His smile was infectious. His voice was enticing and his spirit and personality were totally intriguing. His body was fierce. All together, he was simply beautiful.

But today, I just saw him. Everyone else was getting the lipstick out plotting there plan of seduction. I hid in the back feeling unbeautiful trying to get through the day, reminded myself that I was there to get trained.

-GRACE-

He came to the break room; and yes, he was beautiful. All I could say was, "Where's that smile." He looked at me in an odd way, yet he smiled and walked away. Over and over, I would see the young and old women complement and offer things to try to get a grasp on him. Everyday, he made a point to let me see his smile. He saw me.

When it was time to leave, he wanted to know what I thought about, what I liked and what I believed in. He saw me. I couldn't believe that in the midst of what I would call my ugliest moment in my life, I felt complete in a smile.

I wasn't looking to be with him. I could care less. I had my own mess to deal with. But, the fact that I wasn't on this far gone island of loneliness or that my life was meaningless is when the ultimate revelation of the inner ME began.

~GRACE~

God spoke to me and said…
Take your strengths and use them now.

He said, "The reason why you are so low on your virtue (and the enemy has been able to make you feel inferior to your present circumstances) is because you have done nothing with what I have already given you."

You have great talent.
What have you done to explore and expand in it?

You have great creativity.
What have you done to unleash your creativity?

You have great knowledge.
What have you done to share the abundance of your wisdom?

You have great passion.
What have you capitalized on that feeds and fuels your purpose?

You have great compassion.
What have you done to share with your fellow man that they are not alone?

You have heart.
What have you done to share the love of the Lord?

You give true love.
What have you done to show trueness of love and protection towards yourself?

~GRACE~

You have loyalty.
What ideas/dreams do you have that you are loyal to?

You have deep commitment.
What have you done to show your commitment in the things of God and towards your faith in you?

The main reason that these sentences are worded this way is because you must realize the order in which your focus must lie:

GOD
YOURSELF
FAMILY
MINISTRY/ CAREER
OTHERS

God revealed to me that the problem is that sometimes we let people, places and even things get in the way of our view. We get caught up in the hype of what others need, what must be done or what they think. Where do you really fit in that picture?

Are you so busy running after *things* to prove that you are worthy?

You need to activate the very essence of you, your strengths, talents, skills and gifts and realize that you are more than worthy and can do more than enough for you and your whole household.

~GRACE~

Your focus must be fine tuned into the things of God. (Positive things) Are you running so hard in ministry that you have no idea what's going on within your on home? Is that how you are about the 'status' you have in life? Is your conversation more about what you do than who you are? What is wrong? Where is the missing link? What can you say about the goodness of the Lord? How about the goodness of life?

Look at yourself and realize that some things you experienced was because of God's grace and mercy. If it had not been for the Lord by your side, what they said would kill you, would have. Those who said they would hurt you, would have. Things that they said you would never get over.... Guess what? YOU DID!!!

-Not by might, nor by power, but by the spirit of God-

You were able to withstand an overbearing situation. You were able to make it through with the knowledge and the leverage to be more than a conqueror. When you are able to help others to overcome by your witness and testimony, you must realize that's when you are a new creation in the Lord. It will show.

You must understand that many of your associates/family that have known you before (Your 'Yes" to God) will try to play tug-of-war with you emotionally, because they don't truly understand your changing. Also, they don't want to look in the mirror and deal with or see where they to must also make a change. So now, they are trying to make you feel bad about cleaning up the mess in your life.

Remember: misery loves company

When you start to develop a 'want' a 'hunger' for God and the things of God, You will begin to address things differently around you. You can address and avoid things that you never thought that you could handle. Now, you can see clearly who is for you and who is against you; but more so, who you are.

Hallelujah!

Understand that because of your growth, now is not the time for you to come up against everyone and try to prove to them how much 'In God' you are.

With each stage of growth there is always something new. There are higher heights and deeper depths within each new level of growth. That's why you must realize that no matter how anointed you are, there are times that you still go through. As long as you are in this flesh, you will have some types of trials and tribulations.

The greatness in it all is to know that you know that you serve a God that is all knowing, magnificent and never forsaking. He fights your battles – for it is not your fight to fight it is Gods.

So when you are stressed and don't know which way is up, know that you serve a God that is Alpha and Omega, the beginning and the end, the Creator of all things. If God would take care of the birds in the trees and the blades of grass, then how much more would he care for you? No matter what may come your way, just like Job, God has bragged on you. He sees you for 'The You' that you truly are. God does not see you as what everyone else is trying to get you to be. He knows what he made. Even as you stumble, he ensures that the lesson in your stumbling will be for His glory and will heal and help others. There's more to this than meets the eye. It is about your spirit and who's in control: Others or God.

-GRACE-

~GRACE~

Let me paint this picture for you

Think about a frying pan...
Let's say that you are frying chicken and now it's time for you to take it out.
Each step can be seen as a spiritual representation of one's self

The Pan
YOU

Clean **(starting out)**
Before hurt, pain, years of different seed deposits

The Grease
OUTSIDE INFLUENCES

Clean **(starting out)**
The good, the bad, and the ugly

The Chicken
YOUR EXPERIENCES

Meal
The good, the bad, the ugly

The Seasonings
YOUR MEMORIES

Flavor
The good, the bad, the ugly – And the residue it leaves behind

The Heat
YOUR PROCESS

Transformation
The ups & downs – Trials & tribulations

The Time
YOUR CYCLES

Seasons
The ups and downs – Decisions or lack thereof and end results

~GRACE~

Now, cooking is done.

WHEN ENOUGH IS ENOUGH

The Pan
YOU

Dirty
When you feel that you can't come to God, because you need to 'get yourself together' before you do

The Grease
OUTSIDE INFLUENCES

Dirty
When you can actually see: How things/people around you have affected you

The Chicken
Key effects

Meal
Major affects on your life that you can point out – They are obvious. So, you can 'deal' with them and remove them.

The Seasonings
Residue

Flavor
Memories and behaviors that seem to follow you even after you've removed the key effects

~GRACE~

The Heat Process	***Transformation*** How you have changed, because you no longer desire the old stuff. You desire and require new.
The Time Cycles	***Levels of Growth, Wisdom & Maturity*** Ups & downs – The outcome depends on your 'Yes' to God

LET ME TELL YOU WHAT HAPPENS AFTER YOUR "Yes"

God picks you up
He removes you from the stove
When you have peace in the midst of times of trouble…

He takes you to the Unknown
He takes you to get washed and clean. This is the sink which is 'unfamiliar' to you (the pan) since you are use to being used as something that cooks.

As he washes you in the unknown, you start to feel funny and unsure, because of the GRIT on the bottom of the pan. **The GRIT** is what you have done with the after affects of everything that has come in and entered your life. This residue has left a Mark (*scar*) that hinders you until you let go and let God wash you and make you whole by scrapping away the mess.

~GRACE~

This makes you a new creation in God. You are not what you were before your process. Now, you have experiences, wisdom and knowledge in knowing the things that once were are no longer.

Despite you, God kept you, covered you and showed you that there was more to you than you ever knew. He put passion inside of you to encourage others and a desire not to see anyone go through what you went through. You have a greater understanding about the bigger picture of Gods love than you have ever known.

Get clean in the blood of Jesus. That is, the Word of God. God said, "It's finished." So, you can walk boldly and say, "I am a conqueror and the righteousness of God." The key is that you now know what that means.

SAY YES

~GRACE~

God is Love and God loves you.

You are a conqueror in Christ Jesus who strengthens you.

God made you and predestined you to be much more than what you see. Right now, as you are going through don't be distracted by the trees in the forest and not see the blessing within the forest beyond the trees. Jesus died to set us free - not for us to feel bound by anything or anyone in this world. By His stripes you are healed through the hearing of the word and the confession of your soul.

God made you beautiful. He says that you are beautifully and wonderfully made. You are being pressed and in the fire, the purification of one's soul is revealed and the substance of ones-self comes fourth.

You are an awesome Creation of God. Yes, I said Awesome in God. God has called you and those he called, he justified and those he justified, he glorified. You have a vision in you and God is burning off of you those things that may be hindering you and strengthening you in those things that you will need on the path that He has set before you. Think it not strange that you are getting attacked by misuse and mismanagement of the Word and that you are falling sensitive to things that before wouldn't have bothered you as much.

-GRACE-

God is equipping you to do so much more than you ever dreamed. You have a vision inside of you and it is time to go forth and birth it. What is your passion? What drives you? The answer to those questions should give you understanding of the greater picture that God has placed you in and the greater anointing that he is giving you to conquer it. I know that things seem like they are coming apart or that they are coming at you from all directions, but know this God has ordered your steps and he has strategically placed people in and around your life to "set you up" and push you into your destiny.

You have to have Faith in what God is telling you in your dreams and through certain people in your life. You must have faith in what the Holy Spirit inside of you is instructing you to do. Faith is the substance of things hoped for and the evidence of things not seen. Look at the forest and not the trees for your blessing is in the land of milk and honey and not in the wilderness.

God did not make you and mold you to fail, he did not bring you this far to faint, and he did not carry you this long to fall. You are blessed. God said give me your life and I will save your whole household. You are blessed in your body, in your mind, in your spirit, in your home, in your family, in your work - in everything you do... YOU ARE BLESSED!!!

-BELIEVE AND RECEIVE THE ANOINTING THAT GOD IS POURING OVER YOU-

~GRACE~

Be renewed, and refreshed, be empowered and restored. BE LOVED -for God loved you before he made the earth. He placed a seed of wealth and promise inside of you before he placed you in your mother's womb. Jesus said, "It's finished;" so that you can say, "I can do all things through Christ who strengthens me." Even as it seems you are walking through the valley of the shadows of death (hell and destruction) you shall fear no evil.

FOR GOD IS THY ROCK, THY PROVIDER, THY HELP & STRENGTH. IN HIM YOU CAN DEPEND.

THE DEVIL IS LIAR!!!
May every stumbling block that is coming your way be a stepping stone towards your destiny.

BE ENCOURGED, FEEL RENEWED, BE STRENGTHENED and KNOW

YOU'RE LOVED

-GRACE-

What's Tied to Your Yes

~GRACE~

IT'S TIME TO 'BOOK' YOUR PROBLEM AND 'ARREST' ITS HOLD ON YOU!

-THE PROCESS-
What is 'burning off' of you?

"One, two, stretch.... Can you feel the burn?" one of my aerobics instructors used to say. "You've got to want it! Go further than you think ... Your body will adapt, overcome and improve."

Just think about those few words. Adapt. Overcome. Improve. Everyone wants to improve something within their lives, but are you willing to adapt to the various situations that it may take to get you there? Have we really overcome our adversities? Or, have we become perfect chameleons that blend in with the atmosphere not wanting to bring too much attention to ourselves or make any waves? Have we become the life of the party when really inside we don't enjoy life at all?

What *vices* have you used to get through?

Vice: A degrading or immoral practice or habit. **2.** In place of; replacing. Acting as deputy or substitute for another. **3.** A personal failing; shortcoming.
B. A defect; flaw

Let's just name a few.
Drugs, alcohol, sex, money...?

Hummmm..... Not you. Guess what, there's more.

Overworking, laziness, overly dependant, controlling, redirecting blame, excuse making, plain old Lying, posing a fraud, leeching (spiritually, financially-money, mentally, emotionally, economically – business dealings), manipulation (with your authority/position – family ties – friendship – relationship –with your own children –even in funding), gossiping, abuse (physical, mental, emotional – so you can make others feel your hurt and nullify yours), vanity, people pleasing…

So many issues, so little time to attack them all; however, these very things may be operating in you, around you or toward you.

Ask yourself: What makes me mad, sad or feel insecure? What takes me from trust to mistrust? What do I allow, that deep within I can't stand?

Let me hit you in the face with something. I'm sure that when you looked at drugs, alcohol and sex some of you proclaimed proudly, "No, not me!"

Example: If you have ever had sex to get something, quiet someone down, pass the time and you had to truly fight with your inner spirit to negotiate within your mind how to convince yourself of your actions - so that you could 'justify it' and go through with it - then SEX or more so PEOPLE PLEASING & THE ILLUSION OF NEEDING A PERSON'S TOUCH is YOUR VICE

Again, *What was TIED to Your Yes* within those situations?

-THE PROCESS-

You see, when we look at TV or society and compare our lives, we tend not to see how far we have gotten off of the path that we should be on. Why are you praying for a husband when you don't even know yourself? No one can complete you. One person towards another should only be a compliment – not completion.

Only GOD can complete you.

What's Tied to Your Yes

[86]

-THE PROCESS-

What has 'marinated' with you?

I can't believe she did that to me?

I can't believe that he would say that about me when he knows my personality/character and that I would never do anything like that?

I can't believe he left me, went to her and takes care of her kids and not his own?

I can't believe my mom treats me like an outcast and my other siblings with love and affection (no matter what they do)?

I can't believe she lied and said this child was mine and it's not?

I can't believe they let me go without any warning and I work twice as much as the folks they're keeping?

I can't believe that I have worked here for (x.) years and trained many and yet I'm still not permanent?

I can't believe that after all my sacrifices, she's still nagging at me to be a man and I have provided, comforted, and stayed in the midst of it all?

I can't believe... He/she lied... He/she cheated... He/she manipulated... He/she stole... from me?

I can't believe that after being a friend to many, a shoulder cry on for some and making sacrifices for others' constantly.... That I have no one to truly lean on, no one is really there for me and I feel all alone?

-THE PROCESS-

[88]

What is it that you can't believe?

_____

Why is it 'eating away' at you?

_____

-THE PROCESS-

Understanding the 'Potter's Touch'

O LORD, you are our Father. We are the clay, you are the potter; we are all the work of your hand.
Isaiah 64:8

Blessed is the man who perseveres under trial, because when he has stood the test, he will receive the crown of life that God has promised to those who love him. When tempted, no one should say, "God is tempting me." For God cannot be tempted by evil, nor does he tempt anyone; but each one is tempted when, by his own evil desire, he is dragged away and enticed. Don't be deceived, my dear brothers. Every good and perfect gift is from above, coming down from the Father of the heavenly lights, who does not change like shifting shadows.
James 1:12-14, 16, 17

A person's words can be life-giving water; words of true wisdom are as refreshing as a bubbling brook.
Proverbs 18:4 (NLT)

-THE PROCESS-

What old 'temptation' is keeping you from your 'right now' revelation?

Are you in the midst, yet ministering?

During this journey, I tossed and turned against flesh and spirit in answering this call on my life and trying to understand God...

God in his awesomeness will make you minister, prophesy, and counsel in the midst of your mess. One day after the Word of the Lord rained down and blessed a young lady that I was passing on the sidewalk; she spoke and said, "You are an Awesome, Prophetess of God!" I quickly tried to correct her and replied, "No, I have the gift, but not the office." In saying that, what I really was saying is that I have the ball, but I'm not a player." She just smiled and said, "I've been praying and through you God blessed me." I replied, "Nothing, but the Lord, but in all of this pray." My doubt wasn't in God, but in me. Then before I could take two steps and turn away, I heard the voice of the Lord so clearly saying, "The reason why you won't answer to the call on your life is because you were hurt by someone operating in it." Oh, my Lord, how scary, but yet true.

Almost four years ago, I had joined this church.

Problem #1: God didn't tell me to join.
Problem #2: I didn't even feel lead to join.
Problem #3: Because the pastors had prayed for me once when I was going through... I kind of felt obligated to join (THE BIGGEST PROBLEM OF ALL).

-THE PROCESS-

Then in a matter of days, I went from new member to a lay member with a call of minister, to Praise Team leader. In less than two weeks from joining, I was now getting the music together for all services and prayer, making transparencies, etc. and even when I felt overloaded then.... Now I'm "called" to be a facilitating minister and prayer intercessor all within the same month because "God was doing a quick work and he said for me to do it." I felt like a whirlwind had come over me and it had. Before I knew it, I was constantly running to church to be in order and on "God's timing" and then put on the spot to preach while being told to pull from my past –not go to scripture or to seek God's face. If it was not what they wanted to hear, then I was 'out of order'.

Yet, actually I was more committed to God and the things of God more than I had ever thought of being in my life. I was committed to what they desired --more than work, husband, children, even myself. (I'm all out of order) Are you racing with religion?

I had a prayer life. I was praying and fasting for everything and everyone, but the one thing I missed was in all of that, I didn't pray to God to see if this was His will for me. I was caught up in not making others uncomfortable and even in the midst saying, "Oh Lord, see my love." My soul would cry out, being drained, my house and family falling apart all for the sake of ministry. Not understanding, God desires to build you up not break you down. The love of God outweighs all things. God's love and purpose for your life would never hinder or harm what he has blessed you with (family, your peace of mind, etc.).

So how you ask did I get caught up in this, well I grew up in a traditional, Baptist, say 'AMEN' only after a sermon or singing– no getting happy or any hand clapping church. There were no singing loud and swaying, speaking in tongues, slaying the spirit, prophets, and apostles, praying without ceasing (without someone dying, being sick or in trouble), spiritual warfare, and laying of hands. All of this was Greek to me. So, to see all of that (supposedly) operating within this church, I did not understand it. Yet, I was hungry to have understanding.

As I have grown in God, I have realized that in all things seek God's face and have your focus and your mind set on the things of God and the Holy Spirit within you will give you the discernment to know what is good and pleasing of God's way and will for your life. I have grown to know that even when given a scripture (for review or to address certain situations), I must study to show myself approved in the ways of learning and living God's Word. I need to know the whole concept and not bits and pieces that can easily be taken out of context. I must, in relaying God's word even in explaining God's principles, give out the 'Full meal' and not 'Picked over remains'.

There comes a time when there is that moment when words can not express how low you are in your virtue; however, you still press on. This unbelievable pause that one takes when they get to this place and ask, "Am I on the right road? I know that others are being blessed, healed, delivered, set-free, renewed and restored --- but why, when I get into my secret place there is an unexplainable void?" I am sure that is how John the Baptist, Moses, and even St. Paul felt at one time. Yet, in the midst of ministry the guiding force is the Love of God.

In life there are times you will have a conversation and someone will be hurting trying to express themselves at one point – mad at another and just giving up in the end. What have you observed? What really is the problem? The reason something affects someone so deeply is the root or after effect. When a comment becomes all out war at home, this is not because of what was said; it is almost always what wasn't said.

I realized something when God started to make me look at me and I mean take a real hard look. It wasn't pretty. What I thought was the problem was not even close. I figured out, if you can pinpoint it and pull it out when you think about your issues; it's not the real problem. – Like the chicken – it's not the chicken that does the real damage its that Grit on the bottom of the pan that we forget about as we try to brush ourselves off and start again with a dirty gritty pan(self).

That is why when you are running low on virtue; it is time to have an inner working revival on yourself realizing that…

The Word of the Lord says,

For unto whomsoever much is given, of him shall be much required...Come unto me, all ye that labor and are heavy laden, and I will give you rest, and the peace of God, which surpasses all understanding, shall keep your hearts and minds through Christ Jesus. God is our refuge and strength, a very present help in trouble. With him is wisdom and strength, he hath counsel and understanding. In the day when I cried thou answered me, and strengthened me with strength in my soul. The Lord stood at my side and gave me strength, so that through me the message might be fully proclaimed. But they that wait upon the LORD shall renew their strength; they shall mount up with wings as eagles; they shall run, and not be weary; and they shall walk, and not faint.

For those God foreknew he also predestined to be conformed to the likeness of his Son, that he might be the firstborn among many brothers. And those he predestined, he also called; those he called, he also justified; those he justified, he also glorified. What shall we then say to these things? If God be for us, who can be against us? "Rejoice in that day and leap for joy, because great is your reward in heaven. Rejoice in the Lord always: and again I say, Rejoice. This is the day which the LORD hath made; we will rejoice and be glad in it, because greater is he that is in you, than he that is in the world. Surely goodness and mercy shall follow me all the days of my life: and I will dwell in the house of the LORD for ever. AMEN

-THE PROCESS-

Above Text Was From:

Luke 12:48; Matthew 11:28; Philippians 4:7; Psalms 46:1; Job 12:13; Psalms 138:3; Timothy 4:17; Isaiah 40:31; Romans 12:1-2; Romans 8:31; Luke 6:23; Philippians 4:4; 1 John 4:4; Psalms 118:24; Psalms 23:6

MEN and WOMEN of GOD, called and chosen for such a time as this, please understand that nothing can attack, block or hinder you without God's approval. This is to 'make you' not break you, to mold, mend and shape you into that Creation of Kingdom Destiny that He strategically placed you here for.

May the Blessings of God be *Everflowing* within your ministries, as you walk through the VISION which God made provision before the beginning of the world.

Hallelujah!!!

What processes have you gone through?

-THE PROCESS-

What's Tied to Your Yes

[98]

How did you change?

-THE PROCESS-

What did it bring out of you that you never knew?

How did 'your processes' make you a better person?

-THE PROCESS-

Why

Why I cry
As a child running to hide from the sea of pain when mom left dad

Why I cry
As a heart breaks and aches from love lost or lust gone bad

Why I cry
As the trials come and the tears and fears throughout my years seem to over take me

Why I cry
When from deep inside I know that my why is a deeper reality

I was created for praise and worship with skills and knowledge beyond my grasp
From the dust and wind He molded and mended me again as 'The Potter' continues to sharpen my flask

Before I was placed inside the womb he kept me
Concealed me from sin and shame
He poured in talents, gifts, hope, skills, and a promise that I'll never be the same

For my glory, my purpose
For destiny He calls

-THE PROCESS-

So that as I persevere I continue to hear His voice through it all

To walk boldly, speak confidently even through trials, test and proclaim
I can rejoice; because, I have a Father who loves me just the same

-WHY-

Have you ever asked why? Have you ever wept why? Have you ever just thought why? Haven't we all for whatever reason asked the question hoping for an answer or really some solution to put an end to the stress and pain. Why?

How about why not? Why not you go through? Why? Who else do you think will do? Why not? I'm not trying to push you away, just giving you insight to what has and what will be and what is to come. The even impending 'why' will always remain. However, the point is to not get stuck in why?

-THE PROCESS-

What if:

Moses said 'why me' and stayed at the question why when God said to tell Pharaoh let my people go.

What if:
Daniel said to himself 'why me' in standing for what he believed and disregarded the God he served because of threats of being thrown in the lions den.

What if:
Job cursed God yelling 'why me' after he lost everything he ever loved and owned. Being tormented with illness himself and with his own friends saying that he must have sinned because of what was going on.

What if:
Ruth had a 'why me' in her spirit after losing her husband and being left in a foreign land with her mother-in-law, and instead of going back to her home land (what's familiar – what is an easier decision to make) she continued to be steadfast with helping and supporting her mother-in-law.

What if:
David asked 'why me' after being left alone outside with the sheep while the rest of the family are clean, pampered and becoming well known and it seems as though he's not even noticed.

What if:
Jesus stopped at 'why me' when having to see the world, the people, the values, the immorality and the fickleness and knowing he was laying down his life for not only them, but you and I.

-PAIN-

The pain of being alone, thinking that you're not loved, and feeling as though there's no way out, there is always a way out.

God always gives you a window out of every situation. No matter how messy the situations are that we get ourselves in, remember that you always have a choice. In everything you do, there is a way out (a choice must be made). Usually it is one that is unknown to you. This may bring about fear in you, because you are use to how you've dealt with things in the past. You've experienced your situations before or circumstances that may be similar. You know what excuses you may or may not use to address the circumstance. You have cataloged how and when to react, and you even know when you're defeated. So, venturing into the unknown, not knowing where you're going to stay... Not knowing where you're going to work... Not knowing where your next meal is... Hummm, kind of scary isn't it?

~THE PROCESS~

What's Tied to Your Yes

In prayer and supplication your answers will be given. However, your answers may not always come in the way you may want them or expect them to come.

Walking with integrity and not fear will get you further than any tall tale or bold face lie could ever do. The favor of truth gives you no reason to hide or feel ashamed. The favor of knowing yourself and not trying to conform to what others think is worth more than any silver or gold.

In doing this, you will have restful nights that will outweigh the restless ones.

-THE PROCESS-

Where has running (away from your hurt and problems) gotten you?

Where does your misplaced Anger... Regret lie?

Just Think: Repent not Resent.
Move on!!!
You can never get to your destination thinking about who cut you off in the parking lot.

~THE PROCESS~

-Looking Back-

Lord, what a journey. When I think about my experiences, my dreams, my goals, my beliefs, I can only shake my head at the many twists and turns you've brought me through.

I understand with each dawning day that my life is filled with a universe of experiences that have taken me to continents and countries of life learning impressions, fields of dreams, cities of hope, valleys of retrospect, detours and crossroads of decision, mountains of memories, oceans and seas of thought that peak, drift, fade and return again all to shape and mold this mound of clay that you continuously pour into. Your rain of impartation constantly fertilizes this soil and nurture the seeds within to grow, bloom and bless others in season and out.

I smile, because my view of life had not always been this window of wonder. As I look back and think about how I viewed life then, I just saw this constant revolving door to pain, manipulation, doubt, insecurities and disappointments. I was so busy comparing my life that I lost complete focus on enjoying mine and sharing yours.

Lord, I pray for mankind, your whole creation, because it is all beautiful, glorious and filled with wisdom and peace. Yet, as your children, we have spread our toys far and wide, told tall tales and continue to play games to pass time. We are still writing our dreams with crayon, having our temper tantrums and leaving our mess out for others to endure and clean up. Funny how, we marvel at the independence and success of others. Yet, we quietly allow situations to keep us in an intoxicating dependence towards things/people that have no possibility in prospering us.

I laugh now even as I write, because you make life worth living. Your instructions for living this life are very simple. You desire for us to be wise and be complete in knowing you, loving you, praising you and speaking of you. We just don't want to follow these instructions to the fullness. Just like buying a product, putting it together and when it doesn't come out quite right - complaining about the outcome when all you had to do was follow the instructions. God left us the perfect manual –The Holy Bible.

When you give me these metaphors and analogies, I'm reminded of:

The Fig Tree - Matthew 21
(Some things need to die off in your life.)

The Tree planted by the river - Psalms 1
(What is nurturing your life?)

The Vine and the branches – John 15
(How fruitful are you?)

The Bread and the wine – John 6
(What is Tied to you?)

~THE PROCESS~

My Lord, as I bow before you in humbleness, I thank you for peace. I don't know so many things about my outcome or different dramas in my life. (The why's and why not) However, I understand that these trials show up on my journey as stop signs, detours, billboards, traffic-jams and crossroads. Even though I may not know exactly how things will come to be on the journey of purpose that you've destined for me...

Did Ruth, Moses, Abraham or David?...

All of them had unique beginnings, trying and turbulent midways that lead to an exalted ending for your people and your glory.

I think it not strange that my true revelation has come now after all the battle scars, lies, hurt and pain. I know that I am yet still in the press towards greatness.

When I look back, I remember how things affected me, but I can't conjure up the depth of the actual pain. I see where I pressed when I should have pulled back. I see when I spoke when silence was keen. I even see when I stayed in situations longer than I needed too.

Life lessons and strengths I truly have now. I have seen your glory and have felt your touch of unconditional, unwavering, fatherly love that is not tainted, confusing, convicting or deceiving, but purer than anything this world could ever give me.

-THE PROCESS-

Inspiration

Nothing, but Jesus

Jesus, Jesus, Jesus
There is healing in the name.
There is peace in the name.
There is joy and deliverance in the name.

Jesus,
The solid rock I stand; all other ground is sinking sand.

Jesus,
I rejoice!!!
In the knowledge, the relationship, the promise, in knowing the Lord.

In Him and with Him all things are possible

Hallelujah!

-THE PROCESS-

The Lord is always activating and stirring up gifts and talents. Usually what you see is what you get; however, a child of God is always seeing bigger and broader views.

We all have talents, skills and abilities that are seen each and everyday. As we grow and experience life, God pulls out more things from within that far surpasses anything we had yet to experience. God knows what he created us for as well as what he placed within us for His glory and divine will.

Once we truly decide to 'die to self' and not try to figure it out, the Lord will blow your mind. God says, "My thoughts are not your thoughts neither are your ways my ways."

Trust in the Lord

[113]

~THE PROCESS~

-REVELATION-
Realize your authority and the power within

Beautifully Unique

One day, I was browsing through a brochure of distinctive homes. The name alone makes you give respect and admiration before you even see the first entry. Distinctive (to set apart; to distinguish) isn't that something. As I turned the pages, there it was.

Beautifully Unique, it says with pictures of elegance and awe below, and it goes on to say this:

Located within a private, gated community of only 8 homes. This country French style home is surrounded by beautiful landscaping. This property includes a free form pool and spa, a koi pond, and garden with wonderful views. Spacious interior is appointed in oak and mahogany inlay flooring, and arched mahogany windows and doorways. Dramatic popular beams from a 100 year old barn and Tennessee fieldstone floor enhance the keeping room, and adjoining kitchen, which boasts granite countertops, appliances by Sub Zero and Thermador, and gorgeous washed cabinetry. Two limestone fireplaces accent the formal living room and the banquet sized dining room. The library has a stone accent wall, mahogany bookcases, and rich mahogany paneling. A private sitting area and a dramatic bath with dual vanities, a deluxe shower, a jetted tub, and a large closet are highlights of the master suite. Two staircases lead to the upper level, which is complete with loft area, a computer room, and 4 additional bedrooms. An unfinished bonus above the 3-car garage could serve as an excellent media room or in-law suite. In a sought after community, this home is a true masterpiece. Adjacent three acre estate lot is available to extend your property or build your own dream estate.

What a picture that has been painted. You can actually visualize every step within that home. The elegance, the splendor, the comfort and even the possible price range. Think about the time it took to go through the home and really observe it and take in it's characteristics, and then put the right words together to envelope you and make you feel as through you are right there looking feeling touching and picturing yourself living right there within the 'true masterpiece'.

Imagine what possibilities you could reach, see and explore if you looked at yourself as that distinctive, elegant, regal, filled with splendor masterpiece for all to stop, look, take notice and most of all respect. Think of the reverence we truly would have if we picture our Lord and Savior in that same light.

How do you start seeing yourself the way God sees you?

Write out the adjectives and phrases to best answer these questions below. -- Not what you think others would say or even what you may think now – Pull from within... What do you desire to be? Look deep within your heart and see the treasures from within you.

The outside – What's your atmosphere

Where are you located? What surrounds you and is part of you that can inspire and give warmth?

_____
_____
_____
_____
_____
_____
_____
_____
_____
_____
_____
_____
_____
_____
_____
_____
_____

-REVELATION-

What's your exterior?
What is your landscaping?
What comes in your package that shines first and far most?

-REVELATION-

[118]

What's your interior?

Now, this is where we really get descriptive. This is where we pull out our best of the best. This is where you describe your talents, laugh, skin, heritage, beliefs, outlooks, skills, and aspirations. Everything shines. Everything! Even your lessons in life shine, this is where you SHINE! SHINE! SHINE! Now, pull us all in to stand back, stop and take notice at the beautiful sight you are to see from the inside out.

-REVELATION-

What can be improved? What are your upgrades?

This is so wonderful, because we will always need work in every aspect of our lives. With this continuous journey in life, we gain wisdom as we seek knowledge, notice change, and accept growth. We are always an unfinished work that is to be admired, respected, acknowledged and knows that there's always room for improvement. Even as we speak of the improvements being made, we speak in the positive outstretching of advancement and building. We should always expand our views, open our range and not box in something that was never meant to be caged.

-REVELATION-

Again, as you write and paint your distinctive picture which masterfully describes 'The You' that was always meant to be framed admired and on display, (not covered up, tainted or altered) understand that every great work takes time and effort to take in and really realize what you're holding on to. This is your time to reflect and understand what a valuable asset and prime statue of a person you are. Decide what words of description would be best to bring those things out to present to the world and most of all to you.

REMEMBER:

We are instruments within this orchestra of life. Sometimes our notes may be off key or may seem out of place until you allow God to pull you in and play your part. You then realize that your part is key and unique to the melodies others may bring. In being your best you, the symphony of music played is more beautiful than anything you have ever imagined or heard.

Play <u>Your</u> Part!

Let <u>Your</u> Glory Shine!

-REVELATION-

What's Tied to Your Yes

[121]

Now, Paint Your Portrait.

_____
_____
_____
_____
_____
_____
_____
_____
_____
_____
_____
_____
_____
_____
_____
_____
_____
_____
_____
_____
_____
_____
_____

~REVELATION~

My Heart and Belief in Me now and in You

When I think about the objective for this book, I can only say to you that it was me being obedient to the voice of the Lord putting in what He allowed to help and heal those that this book was meant to bless.

In my heart, I pray that after this you can review your steps – resolve some issues and begin in movement manifesting things within your life that were meant to bless not only you, but also those in which you will come in contact with.

Knowledge begins that drop in the water and the ripples are the after effects, revelations and outward impartations that you influence through your wisdom, experience and spirit.

My prayer for you is that you see through the mention of David, Ruth, and Peter that trials come and go and the true test is how you overcome and see the unseen and become that in which you couldn't have ever dreamed to be.

I share with you not only my experiences, but my heart. My past doesn't make me. It might have pruned, purged, and cut-off things around me and on me. Who I am now and who I will be was here before the heavens. I am living without worry. I am worshiping, praying, and enjoying all that God has prepared before me.

I leave you with a prayer of repent as I went through. This prayer I prayed when I finally came to the revelation of YES!!

~MY FINGERPRINT~

What it meant and where I was in the process. You can see me now, because of the journey, because of the walk, because of the path that was set before I ever came to be.

Here you have shared my fingerprint.

Don't let this world go without seeing yours.

What was tied to My YES?...

Lord,
It's me coming to you as humble as I know to FULLY and TOTALLY submit myself to you. My will, my way, my yesterday no longer exists for in you Lord, God I'm whole. In you Lord, God I'm set free. In you Lord, God I'm victorious, a conquer and not of this world but in this world.

I have come short of God's glory, but that does not mean that the enemy will prevail. The Devil is liar and my God the creator of the heavens and the earth is not a man that he would lie.

I bind these Spirits that have been trying to hinder me and keep me from fulfilling my promise in the mighty name of Jesus.

Pride, Envy, Deceit, Control, Jealousy, Manipulation, Depression, Fear, Timidity, Self pity, Self doubt, People pleasing, Selfishness, Judgmental, Liar, Double mindedness, Confusion, Distraction, Temptress, Hold grudges, Sexual perversion and Falsehood

In the name of Jesus take away every hindering spirit and cast them down to the depth of hell, In Jesus' Name and loose in the earth and heaven:

Love, Patience, Kindness, Self-discipline, Keen discernment, Sound Mind, Revelation knowledge, One mind, Wisdom,

What's Tied to Your Yes

Grace, Peace, Mercy, Joy, Hope, Honesty, Loyalty and Truth, Truth, Truth!!!
In the name of Jesus.

Lord, please forgive me of my sins, the many lies, cover ups misleading ways, disregard for authority, disrespect, dishonesty and how I would allow sex to fill voids which left me empty and cold.

You guided me to scriptures and checked my spirit; yet, I turned away and not out of lack of love for you, Lord. But, I had no love and belief in me. I almost couldn't accept the peace and time alone that you blessed me with. I almost messed it all up. Even when I would accomplish things, I would find something wrong. I could not enjoy or even celebrate me. Forgive Me.

I do say Yes, to you Lord. I have realized that even as I truly say it from my soul it is so much better than the years, days, months and minutes before. I must pray to you and stay focused.

Again, Lord, forgive me for disobeying you. I desire to be all that you have called me to be. Before the foundation of the earth, before my mom met my dad, before the Cross when you were creating the heavens and we all sat at your feet. Lord, just to think of your awesomeness and your goodness, I'm in awe. I know that you've covered and that you've kept me.

~MY FINGERPRINT~

[126]

Lord, wash me, refine me and make me new. Please, wash the murk from my cup and remove the residue from my spirit and soul.

Lord, I pray for healing and prosperity over my life and my whole household. I release the hurt, pain and shame of my yesteryear including up to this very second. I am not worthy of your love or even the call upon my life, but I accept it humble and broken before you.

Yes, Lord to be honest, I wondered why and how does my relationship with my parents still affect me today.

I pondered over why am I in my mom's home when I've worked hard all my life never to be. I see your divine favor upon others and even though I smile at the blessing (I ask in my heart – why not me?) Forgive me, Lord. You place people in my life and they challenge your Word and my faith in you (I want to have judgment in my heart) Forgive me, Lord. You have shown me distractions that I have allowed to detour me from where I am suppose to be. (I'm so sorry, Lord)

Help me, Father to be saved again in your divine will and way for my life. Lord, I love you. You hold me and you've rocked me to sleep when I was restless. You provided for me when I had not a clue. Lord, you cleared my mind when it tried to go mad. You wiped the tears and mended my heart when I was sad and lost.

~MY FINGERPRINT~

I can hear, speak, walk, sing and dance. How dare I complain! Your love is so unconditional and not like man. When I feel alone, you say I'm not. When man says I'm nothing, you say, "Yes, you are everything and much more." Lord, nothing compares to you.

Remove every hindrance, I seek you Lord, not just because I'm broken, but because Lord truth be told I'm a mess -in mess- yet you said that to call on your name, to seek and I shall find, to knock and the door will be opened, to walk and not faint and I pray to you, Lord. I ask of you to fix me, mend me, mold me, hold me and show me.

Oh, Lord even now, you are so wonderful and marvelous. In your name Jesus, forgive me and show me how to walk this walk. Let my eye and discernment be keen in things of you and things not of you. Lord, please teach me!!!

And God's Word speaks

(For Me)
Teach me your way Oh Lord, and I will walk in your truth, give me an undivided heart, that I may fear your name. I will praise you, Oh Lord, my God with all my heart; I will glorify your name forever. For great is your love toward me: you have delivered me from the depths of the grave. The arrogant are attacking me, O God and band of ruthless men seek my life – men without regard for you.

[128]

But you, O Lord, are a compassionate and gracious God slow to anger abounding in love and faithfulness. Guide me in your truth and teach me, for you are God my Savior and my Hope is in you all day long.

Psalms 86:11-15; Psalms 25:5

(From God)
I will give them singleness of heart and actions, so that they will always fear me for their own good and the good of their children after them. I will give them an undivided heart and put a new spirit in them; I will remove from them their heart of stone and give them a heart of flesh.

Ezekiel 11:19

Thank You, Lord

What is tied to Your YES?

~MY FINGERPRINT~

May **Your Ripples** Go Out And Become
Bigger Than Mine

May **Your Influences** Throughout Your
Lifetime Be Bigger Than You

~MY FINGERPRINT~

What's Tied to Your Yes

[131]

-MY FINGERPRINT-

Beloved,

I leave you with this. It's not hard to serve God, but it is hard to live a fulfilled and enriched life without Him.

If you haven't said Yes or you had, yet time, things and circumstances somehow got in the way. It's never too late for God. It's never too late for you.

You don't have to know all the answers or any answers or have yourself together to come to the Lord and start anew. That's what His unconditional, redeemed, sacrificial love does. It makes the crooked path straight and the broken heart mended.

God never closes the door on you. He never leaves nor forsakes His children.

~MY FINGERPRINT~

Even when you're going through, God knows you have what it takes to make it. So, yes sometimes you may feel lonely and like you can't face what's before you, But God has you and He would never put you in harms way.

So always, look at your steps and the choices you make. Are your steps guided towards destiny and purposes or driven toward destruction and drama? Are your steps of God or of you?

The following is a prayer of praise, reverence, repentance, and renewal. Whenever your road gets rough, pick up this book and know that you have a Father who cares for you.

My prayer for you is for you to continue on the path of realizing who you are. Affirm yourself. Know yourself. Know you're loved and most of all

BLESSED!!!

~MY FINGERPRINT~

LORD,

I come humbly before you. I bow at Your feet.
I leave the past behind and empty myself unto You

Sanctify, purify, refine me and make me whole
I leave behind the pain, hurt, worry and fears of yesteryear
I now resurrect the joy, peace, victory and the divine walk that You Created me

For Your Glory
I exalt Your name and I hear Your call. I magnify Your name and give You praise
I thank You for this minute this very second and this right now moment just to be able to lift Your name as the angels and sing hallelujah, glory, praises and honor unto You. I send perfumes of praise and worship to You
You are the King of Kings, Lord of Lords, my All and All,
The Almighty and All wondrous God, there is none like You

As I Come, I repent before You, for things within my flesh and even my thoughts that have been Unpleasing of You and not of Your Will or Your Way
I thank You for every opportunity and every step that I have taken in You

As I Continue on my journey toward my destiny,
I lift my hands unto You
To be washed and cleansed again in the blood of Jesus

I thank You for your loving kindness, your mercy and grace which kept me even when I didn't want to be kept.

Thank You, for making me an heir to the throne and showing me that You made me in your likeness and that I am fearlessly and wondrously made
I can hold my head high and say that 'I am the righteousness of God' 'I am more than a conqueror' and that 'I am victorious in You'

I thank You for divine placement and strategic meetings that place me where I should be, to be a living witness of Your Glorious Light

As I come, I hold on, even through this life's troubles
To let none of these things separate me from my lifeline which is You
I understand that any ailment that befalls me is just a temporary inconvience
By Your stripes I am healed by the hearing of Your Word and the confession of my soul

I praise you, Oh Lord, the author and finisher of my faith
I can walk knowing and acknowledging that You are not a man that you would lie and that Your word doesn't return to you void.

So when you,

My Father – speak it – It is finished!!!

[136]

I can boldly say that the things of my past are now in the sea of forgetfulness

Now as I come, not knowing how it looks or where it might lead
I am going to stand on Your Word as it gives me foundation and sets my path that leads me to my promise in You

For Your Awesome Glory. I love You and exalt You and Magnify Your Name

In the Mighty Name of Jesus, I Pray

AMEN

What's Tied to Your Yes

[137]

About Our Author:
RitaShay Thomas

Inspirational, empowering and high-energy are just some of the adjectives that you hear being said after hearing Ms. Thomas speak. Whether it is a luncheon or a sanctuary with standing room only, she packs an overwhelming punch of revelation and powerful insights while you laugh, examine God's truths and witness how He uses this vessel through lectures and song to spread His word of life, liberty and peace.

Motivational speaker, author and psalmist, RitaShay Thomas, is a mother of two and a native of Memphis, TN in which she served as a lead vocalist at Olivet Baptist Church with Reverend and Councilman Kenneth T. Whalum, whose son the well-known saxophonist Kirk Whalum was a member. After dealing with the many hands that 'life' dealt her, she is continuing her education in Biblical Studies. With persistence and determination, she has become a Graphic/Interior designer and minister and stands on the scripture of (Luke12:48) to whomsoever much is given, much shall be required.

Ms. Thomas is founder of My Time to Shine Inc., which has started in Atlanta, GA to empower and educate families and communities to think outside of the box and see life in what she has phrased 'The Panoramic'. There are plans to open another location in Memphis, TN. She has also started an outreach ministry via the internet titled: Prophetic Touch which focus is on empowerment and building relational knowledge of God's Word through praise, worship and devotion. She has written many stories, articles and plays for ministries, magazines and after school programs. Since moving to Atlanta, GA in 1998, she has served under: Pastor Paul Bowen, Bishop Wiley Jackson, II, and now Bishop Eddie L. Long of New Birth Missionary Baptist Church, in praise and worship, outreach ministries, and counseling.

Rita's passion can be summed up as "Empowerment and Awareness". She speaks to high school students as well as congregations about the promises and revelations of God's purposes for one's life. She has been vital to Women's Ministries in helping to pull out that 'Proverbs 31 Woman' that God created. She stands in the gap to pray and counsel many that have gotten caught up in the world's ways and leads them to the joy, peace and understanding of God's planned and predestined life of victory that is for us all.

For information on book signing, conference speaking, other products or promotions please contact: www.MyTimeToShine.org

Blessed to be a Blessing

Prophetic Touch Empowerment will like to thank you for your purchase of 'What's Tied to Your Yes!' We want to enable everyone to experience the love of God in an awesome and renewed way. Our specials are in place to spread God's Word and also express our happiness in your continued growth and knowledge of the Agape Love of the Lord.

Special Offers

(Valid only through Prophetic Touch Empowerment & My Time To Shine)

2 books for $25	[over 15% off of the retail price]
10 books for $100	[over 25% off of the retail price]
25 books for $225	[over 35% off of the retail price]
100 books for $800	[over 45% off of the retail price]
500+books	**Please email or write us for wholesale pricing.**

Please send check or money order made payable to:

Prophetic Touch Empowerment
c/o Rita Shay Thomas
484 Hillandale Park Drive
Suite 200
Lithonia, GA 30058

Please visit us at:

"Breaking Barriers Through the Word of God"
www.prophetictouch.com